Praise for Gina Ramsey

Page-turning adventure, laughter, and surprises. I am ready for the Gina Ramsey stand-up tour.

**— Andrea Cheydrea, author of
*A Poet's Playground***

I laughed out loud! Gina's stories remind us to find joy and laughter in every corner. Her experiences remind me of so many of my own, and now I reflect on them from a new, silver-lined perspective. This is a great read that can be consumed in bits or as a whole, and it is full of encounters anyone can relate to. Undoubtedly, every reader will start to identify their own *Burnt Glovebox* stories—seeing their calamities (or at least parts of them) as humorous. What a lovely gift Gina is giving the world!

**— Liz Sheahan, BSW, MA,
nonprofit professional**

What a fun and easy read that kept me flipping pages wanting more. I cracked up, laughing out loud throughout the chapters. The enthusiastic writing by the author, Gina Ramsey, made me feel like I was sitting with a great friend and hearing about her life's antics with relatable stories from a fun and colorful perspective.

**— Kristi Davis, entrepreneur and author
of *Redeemed: Guide to SELF-LOVE,
Journey to TRUE HAPPINESS***

A much-anticipated follow-up to the *Burnt Gloveboxes: Embracing Life When It Goes Up in Flames, Volume II* doesn't disappoint. As in the first book, the common thread of the stories is one of mishap mayhem. Gina Ramsey's hilarious tales run the gamut from dealing with an inebriated bathroom bully and an overzealous sales cashier to a road trip from hell involving twenty-four quarts of oil. As an added bonus, some friends share their own quirky stories, underlining Gina's intention to remind the reader of the importance of looking for the positive whenever something goes wrong. *Burnt Gloveboxes: Embracing Life When It Goes Up in Flames, Volume II* is the perfect tonic for our challenging times.

— **Kelly McKenzie, author of *Never, Never, Hardly Ever: A Mother/Daughter Story of Antiques and Antics***

Delighted to get my hands on this new volume of *Burnt Gloveboxes*! There is nothing better than humorous, all-too-relatable stories to boost my mood on a dreary day! Gina's entertaining and propulsive writing style makes the pages just fly by as you dive into her various madcap adventures. I dare you to try and read just one story!

—**Jacki Rykal, book enthusiast**

Gina Ramsey delivers yet another hilarious collection of stories in *Burnt Gloveboxes Volume II*! Readers will love her perspective and philosophy on life—to find the funny even in tough situations. Gina has a stellar ability to tell humorous, captivating stories about her comical everyday life. *Burnt Gloveboxes Volume II* is a fun, mood-boosting read perfect for anyone who needs a good laugh. Gina's joy in life and ability to make the most of all situations are contagious. I can't wait to read more in future volumes!

— **Lisa Kielty, an avid reader and lover of books**

The whisperer of all things wacky, Gina Ramsey, has done it again! Behold the second installment of *Burnt Gloveboxes*, a book that'll have you saying, "No way You didn't? You did!" while tears roll down your legs. So, strap on your most absorbent adult diapers, and get ready to tinkle with joy and amusement as we all laugh at Gina and more of the inconceivable moments that seem to seek her out, if for no other reason than our reading pleasure.

— **Shelli Ragle, humorist, speaker, and writer**

Burnt Gloveboxes II

Also by Gina Ramsey

Burnt Gloveboxes: Embracing Life When It Goes Up in Flames

Burnt Gloveboxes II
Embracing Life When It Goes Up in Flames

Gina Ramsey

Foreword by
Kathy Kinney

Edited by
Deborah Kevin

HIGHLANDER
PRESS

BURNT GLOVEBOXES II. Copyright © 2025 by Gina Ramsey

ISBN: 978-1-956442-51-9
Ebook ISBN: 978-1-956442-52-6
Library of Congress: Applied for.

Published by
Highlander Press
501 W. University Pkwy, Ste. B2
Baltimore, MD 21210

Editor: Deborah Kevin
Cover design: Patricia Creedon
Cover images: Adobe Stock
Author's photo credit: JoAnn Jardine at Studio One Photography

To my family and friends who have shared Burnt Gloveboxes
experiences with me and to Burnt Gloveboxes fans:
Thank you for your ongoing love and support.

Contents

Vacation Miscommunication

Burnt Glovebox Community Stories

Disclaimer

The essays in this book are nonfiction. All my stories and the stories written by the *Burnt Gloveboxes* community contributing authors are based on memory and depicted as truthfully as possible.

While all persons depicted in the stories are actual individuals, some names and identifying characteristics have been changed to respect their privacy.

If you granted me permission to use your actual name—for instance, if you're a family member, friend, coworker, or former coworker—I have only used your first name.

If you are offended by this, I genuinely apologize. I did this because I love you and want to protect you from the possibility of paparazzi flooding your front lawn for weeks on end, snapping unauthorized photos of you when the *Burnt Gloveboxes* series becomes a cultural craze.

Foreword
Kathy Kinney, actor and author

If you've ever had things go sideways in your life, and I know you have, Gina Ramsey leads a master class in surviving life's pitfalls by finding the funny nugget of wisdom in the absurd, the chaotic, the random encounters, and the bizarre experiences we all encounter on this wacky journey called life.

It turns out that finding the funny is a superpower, and wielding that power just might be the difference between staggering through life and riding an inner tube down the whitewater rapids of a fast-moving river while throwing your head back and howling with joy.

Gina Ramsey's *Burnt Gloveboxes II* will make you smile, chuckle, snort, and nod in agreement as she guides you through a myriad of experiences that are so relatable you'll be asking yourself if Gina is psychic. Nope, she's just a brilliant observational humorist with a knack for finding the funny in life.

Introduction

 If you think you are too small to make a difference, try sleeping with a mosquito.

— *Dalai Lama*

Throughout my adult life, I have been meandering, searching for my place in this world. For as long as I can remember, I've pondered, "What is my purpose? What will bring me happiness? Do I have a gift, and if so, what is it? Am I capable of making a difference in the lives of others and our world?" There have been countless times I have felt lost, endlessly pursuing answers to my questions to no avail.

My indecisiveness captured the essence of the phrase, "jack-of-all-trades, master of none." My career choices and college track record have been diverse, to say the least. For example, at one point, I wanted to be a zoologist to help animals. This came shortly after seeing Dian Fossey's story of moving in with primates in the movie *Gorillas in the Mist.*

On my first day at Intro to Zoology, the instructor pointed at some glass cases with black-winged creatures crawling around. "You see these cute little guys? They need to be cared for. You must sign up to come into the classroom one night each week at 8 p.m. to open the encasements so they can fly around the classroom to get some exercise."

Is this seriously a prerequisite to snuggling in the jungle with silverbacks? Immediately, I envisioned the terrifying scene of one of those black-winged hamsters getting snagged in my eighties back-combed "big hair." The next day, I withdrew my class registration.

After working at several low-paying jobs, I decided to "officially" go to college at thirty-one. My major? Pharmacy, nursing, chemistry …

The ongoing changing of majors became a running joke. One Christmas, family members wore red, foam clown noses to the family gathering, asking if I had signed up for clown school. They suggested all the possibilities of this prestigious career, stomping around in over-sized shoes, zooming around in tiny cars, and sporting the newest fashions in colorful makeup and clothing. I found this hysterical.

My ongoing irresolution was bringing me familial fame, and I loved it. My husband, Paul, was lucky enough to be on the crazy train of quirkiness with me. In all reality, I was fortunate he remained on board. As for our kids, Jackie, Mike, and Katie, they had no choice. They rode along, and we hoped they would learn valuable lessons along the way.

At one point, Paul tried to help me find my path during a trip to Walt Disney World. After hearing me repeatedly obsess over my dream of working at Disney Animation Studios, he asked a cast member for an application. He handed it to me, saying, "I want you to pursue your dreams."

Having an issue with being told what to do, I drew the line. I refused to pursue a career in animation just because he thought it would be a good fit for me! In reality, I doubted my ability to paint cartoon figures and never filled out the application. I've had several moronic episodes during my life. This was one of them, given I forwent an opportunity for possible free theme park admission.

Finally, I settled for a degree in graphic design since the animation and clown industries didn't seem promising. However, after I proudly marched to the tune of "Pomp and Circumstance," I found my circumstances unfavorable. I could not secure employment in my field but found a position helping individuals in need to find community resources.

After a few years, I decided it was in my best interest to keep racking up student loan debt to advance myself professionally. This is what we are supposed to do, right? After three years in a master's degree program, I marched to the same collegiate tune. I have been a social worker ever since.

It wasn't until I reached the age of fifty-three that I discovered I had been on the correct path and fulfilling my purpose during my entire journey. I was making a difference without realizing it. The many roadblocks life presented to me, and the winding paths I chose were blessings in disguise, as these led me to discovering my treasured gift.

Some reference encountering a barrage of unfavorable scenarios and circumstances by the adage of Murphy's Law: "Anything that can go wrong will go wrong." However, I realized there is a missing component: the importance of "finding the funny" or looking for the positive when something goes wrong. I've coined this motto as "Burnt Gloveboxes." I created this title based on a previous experience that left the door charred. (See *Burnt Gloveboxes: Embracing Life When It Goes Up in Flames*, Volume I.)

Looking at life through the lens of humor and positivity has been my gift during the entire journey. Little did I know the positive impact I made by sharing my stories with others.

In addition, my aspirations of writing a book resonated with so many of my friends and family. During the times I felt I was not living a life of purpose, they were in the background cheering me on, knowing I had the drive and potential to share happiness and a positive mindset with our world.

One of these cheerleaders was Hannah E. B. However, I didn't learn of her support until I began writing my first book, with the goal of creating an anthology where others would share their own *Burnt Gloveboxes* stories.

I called my best friend Julie and asked, "Hey Jules, do you remember that rat story you told me years ago? Would you be willing to write that story for the book?"

She responded, "Hannah wrote the story way back when the incident happened. I'll try to find it for you."

After a quick search, she found not only the treasured story but much more. At eight years old, Hannah put her pen to paper and wrote her version of the rat story.

The most remarkable thing was Hannah's letter that accompanied her rat tale. This little girl heard me talk about my vision of one day writing a book. In the postscript of her letter, she included her encouragement, saying, "I hope you write your book someday."

Amazingly, Hannah believed in me before I believed in myself. Her words are a testament that I have been fulfilling my purpose by finding the funny/positivity in life's mishaps and encouraging others to do the same. Her beautiful words confirmed I have been making a difference in our world all along.

Several people approached me with their own stories of Murphy's wrath. You will find a couple of these stories, including Hannah's story, toward the end of this second edition of *Burnt Gloveboxes*. I hope these tales of mishaps, conundrums, and some poor decisions spark a smile and encourage you to reflect on your encounters with Murphy through a lens of positivity.

Finally, if you are a fellow indecisive soul aimlessly searching for a way to make a difference in our world, know you are in good company. I encourage you to keep trudging forward, knowing others are cheering you on from the sidelines. At some point, you will believe in yourself, just as they believe in you.

How May I (Not) Help You?

If you'd like to press 1, press 3. If you'd like to press 3, press 8.
If you'd like to press 8, press 5.

— *Glasbergen*

Two things can impact the customer experience at any business: the demeanor of the front-line customer service workers and the decisions made by the business owners.

There are valued businesses in our communities. The employees and management provide a positive and memorable experience despite numerous encounters with rude or unruly customers. Most customer service workers move past these negative encounters, remaining dedicated to treating the next customer with kindness and a smile.

However, some customer service workers ride the Train of Misery. They aim to snag happy-go-lucky customers and drag them aboard the train as it moves down the rail tracks of impending doom at lightning speed. They cunningly brainwash each customer with their doom-and-gloom agenda of monotone verbal sarcasm and nonverbal glares and gestures. Finally, the customer is violently shoved off the moving train, lands in the ditch, and wonders, *What just happened?*

Another factor impacting the overall customer service experience is decisions made by top executives to "increase efficiency and profitability." Substandard decision-making by the powers that be is likely a reason their employees are on the Train of Misery in the first place. To make things worse, these decisions sometimes cause customer distress and anger. Take a bag of chips, for example. The leaders of potato chip companies decided they can trick us, and we fall for it every time. We now purchase a massive bag with only ten chips inside. What a scam! (I know you are shaking your head in agreement.)

Luckily, some marvelous stories result from the crappy service and poor corporate decisions. Let's review a few examples of "How may I (NOT) help you" scenarios.

The Sales Pitch

 Upsell: an attempt to convince a customer to purchase something additional or more costly.

— *Merriam-Webster*

LITTLE DID I KNOW THAT FINDING EMPLOYMENT AS A GRAPHIC designer would be highly challenging when I graduated from college. Well, in my case—IMPOSSIBLE. Most job postings required at least five years of experience, which I did not have as a recent graduate, and the small town we lived in was far from being a mecca for booming design agencies.

My good friend Julie, whom I met during college, also had difficulty finding a job. After several unsuccessful attempts to find employment in her field of study, she landed a job as a women's advocate at The Women's Community in Wausau, Wisconsin. After hearing my job search woes, she told me the agency was hiring and suggested I apply. Thankfully, I got hired!

The team I worked with was fun and loved to joke around, tell stories, and laugh—a coping mechanism that kept us all trudging along and returning to the office day after day. Diving into the trenches and hearing daily recounts of traumatic experiences told by individuals affected by domestic and sexual violence and advocating for their safety was emotionally exhausting. To continue the good fight, we needed an outlet, and this was finding a funny each day. My coworker's favorite was my daily morning gas station/convenience store tales.

Each morning, I stopped to pick up a large hazelnut coffee and the story of the day before heading to the office. My purse and coffee would barely hit my desktop before my coworkers gathered at the door, anticipating my latest crazy anecdote.

This popular convenience store chain was a Wisconsinite favorite because it carried an extensive array of items and had friendly service. However, this haven had one downfall: the cashiers ALWAYS attempted to rope customers into purchasing an extra item. The most popular items offered were donuts, cookies, or their special rewards card.

The sales strategies at the store I visited in the mornings became increasingly bizarre. For example, one day, the cashier asked me, "Would you like to purchase some fruit?"

The display table to my left held a large chipwood bushel basket heaped with apples and oranges. The vibrant combination of red, green, and orange and the sweet, fruity smell wafting into the air made this offer tempting, but I decided to decline.

"No, thank you," I said.

She switched tactics and countered using the enthusiastic persuasion method.

"But they are only three for a dollar; that's a terrific deal!"

"No, thank you. I am not interested in buying any fruit today."

Not taking "no" for an answer, she switched gears to the guilt method, explaining the health benefits of fruit and the importance of consuming this superfood daily.

I felt trapped, standing there nodding like a bobblehead figurine and wondering when the full-length lecture on "The Benefits of Eating Fruit" would end.

She finally ran out of steam and stopped providing the long-winded fruit facts. We moved to an ocular showdown. She stood there. I stood there. Our eyes connected, locked as if she was attempting to convince me to "buy the fruit" via telepathic communication.

With one final "No thank you" from me, she realized her attempts at a fruit sale had failed.

After the produce battle, there were occasions when I paid for my coffee and left the store without a showdown. Not making eye contact or engaging in small talk with the cashier was a short-term prevention against another pitch fest, but it wasn't long before I became "The Chosen One" again.

The cashier asked, "Do you need any cigarettes today?"

I looked at her in disbelief. *Why would she ask me that? Do I look like a smoker?* It amazed me how they changed their sales pitch from the fruit baskets to tobacco products. *Did the fruit-selling lady redo her statistics and realize that more people would rather smoke than eat healthy?*

"No, thank you," I said in disbelief.

At that point, I probably should have chosen another store to purchase my daily caffeine fix, but I didn't, mostly out of curiosity and, if I'm being honest, I didn't want to let my coworkers down. They'd come to relish my convenience store encounters.

What product will they try to sell to me next?

The third time's a charm. I made an afternoon stop to purchase some lunch. I carried my turkey sandwich, potato chips, and a bottle of water to the cashier. Finally, I was purchasing more than a simple cup of hazelnut coffee and believed the cashier would have no reason to upsell. Wrong-o!

I placed my items on the counter. She scanned the bar codes one by one and then asked me, "Would you like to purchase a sandwich today?"

Are you kidding me? I did my due diligence to prevent the sales pressure AND she just scanned my sandwich!

In our previous absurd interactions, I kept to myself, trying to engage as little as possible. Being mindful of the cashier's feelings, I politely declined any attempts to upsell. However, I had hit my breaking point. This insanity had gone on too long.

I looked at the cashier, pointed down at my items, and sheepishly said, "But I already have a sandwich. How many sandwiches should I be eating?"

Not responding, she finished my transaction and, with a smile, stated the last words every customer hears at the end of their shopping experience: "Have a nice day! We'll see you next time."

They have crafted the delivery of this phrase into linguistic sorcery. It places each customer into a hypnotic spell, blankly nodding and saying, "Yes, master," in a monotone voice as they shuffle out the door. The cashiers knew there would always be a next time and another opportunity to attempt an additional sale. This strategy certainly worked with me.

This brilliant and cunning use of the luring exit phrase and the intriguing upsell offers mesmerized me. Clearly, under the cashiers' spells, I continued making my early morning stops to grab a large cup of hazelnut coffee, find out the newest peculiar promotion, and return to my office to provide the daily convenience store report.

Front Desk Preacher

 There's a fine line between a long sermon and a hostage situation.

— *Garrison Keillor*

It was the night before our flight to sunny Orlando, Florida, for a women's week of magical fun at Walt Disney World. My daughter Katie and I arrived at our hotel in Minneapolis, checked in, and reserved a shuttle to the airport the following day.

During the check-in process, the front desk clerk over-explained in minute detail every topic related to our stay, including how to use the room key, how to use the elevator, what time breakfast was served, where it was served, what was being served, and who was serving it. In her defense, the elevator was a bit complicated, so the extra details came in handy.

We carried our luggage to our room and settled in. It was well past dinnertime, and we were famished. We walked to a little grocery store across from the hotel to purchase something to eat, intending to return it to our room.

Upon our return to the hotel, we noticed that the same front desk clerk was conversing with the maintenance worker. We tried to keep to ourselves, but she stopped us to inquire if our room was satisfactory. We confirmed it met our expectations. By simply offering our early five-star room review, we opened a portal. The clerk immediately set her hooks in deep, holding us captive. We were famished, worn out, and trapped without a clear plan to escape.

The maintenance guy asked, "What's the reason for your stay?"

"We are on vacation and flying out of Minneapolis tomorrow morning," I said.

"Where are you two flying to?" he asked.

Excited, Katie and I said in unison, "Walt Disney World."

His icy blue eyes widened as instantaneously as his response, "Wow, that must be expensive."

Stoic, six feet tall and slender, he stood motionless. His laser-beam eyes pierced our souls, awaiting our response.

Katie and I looked at each other, not knowing how to respond, but Katie stepped up and said, "Yes, it can be expensive. We are doing a girls' trip and are looking forward to it."

"Good for you! Good for you!" he said. "You must do things like that from time to time."

The clerk inquired what airline we'd be flying on, and we answered, sharing that we would be on a direct flight into Orlando. Her demeanor shifted, and, like a preacher to her congregation, she proceeded with her sermon, telling us she used to work at Minneapolis airport, and she was familiar with "said airline."

"I'm warning you: they will charge you for a cup of water, so don't order water. Bring bottled water. They will also charge you for paper tickets, so download your tickets onto your phone before arriving at the airport. You need to know that they will charge you for *everything*."

We expressed understanding and thanked her for the information and her deep concern for what we apparently got ourselves into.

She continued to offer the same information repeatedly and enthusiastically to ensure that we fully understood the importance of her messages and the gravity of the situation.

She began each new sentence with, "I'm warning you ..." or "You need to know ...."

We nodded as she continued, trapped in this twenty-minute repetitive information cycle. Our stomachs growled, and the circulation in our fingers was slowly being cut off from the handles of the plastic grocery bags full of food.

The maintenance guy recognized our captive state. He probably saw the blank stares on our faces and realized he needed to do something to help us. He interjected a random statement to divert the one-way airline discussion. I glanced at my watch. It was 10:30 p.m. This was our opportunity to run—and fast.

"Well, we need to get to our room so we can eat and get some rest," I said. Katie followed my lead.

Approving our excuse, the clerk removed the hooks she had set in, releasing us from the captivity of airline banter. We quickly shuffled our way to the elevator, pressed the up button, and glanced back at the desk. Eyes still on us, the clerk stated, in a creepy *Twilight Zone* demeanor, "I'm warning you, download your tickets tonight!" We thanked her as the elevator doors opened, and we made our escape.

The clerk's warnings slowly sank in as the elevator rose. Concerned about the likelihood of extra charges, eating became a secondary priority. I immediately went online to download our tickets to my phone. Though we had booked our flight through Orbitz, I needed to download our digital tickets from the airline's website.

When I logged on and entered our reservation number, the system showed no reservations. Frantically, I typed in all options, attempting to locate our reservation, including my name, Katie's name, and the reservation number again. Nothing.

Next, I attempted to look up the flight, but the airline website did not list our morning flight, even though it still appeared on the Orbitz site. My stomach twisted, and I felt ill. Something was terribly wrong.

A phone call with the Orbitz representative confirmed, "It appears the airline has changed your flight. You will need to contact the airline directly to inquire further."

In disbelief, I remained sitting on the bed, frozen, trying to process what was happening. Katie took over. She called the airline and spoke to a representative who informed her they had changed our flight. The direct flight to Orlando no longer existed. We were now scheduled to fly out of Minneapolis at **10:30 p.m.** the next night instead of 9:30 a.m. We'd then have an overnight layover at Denver airport before flying to Orlando the following day.

WHAT? We have scheduled our resort check-in for tomorrow afternoon, with dinner reservations booked at five o'clock, and we expect our friend Julie to arrive in Orlando tomorrow evening. We can't arrive a day late! My heart raced faster with each thought. Disbelief paralyzed me as the events unfolded.

Katie sternly interrogated the representative in an "Oh, I don't think so!" mode. "Why were we not informed about the flight change?"

The representative said, "We did not have your contact information."

Not falling for that untruth, Katie responded, "You have our contact information. We had to enter it when we ordered the tickets. Changing our flight and not notifying us is unacceptable! You need to reschedule us on a morning flight to Orlando immediately!"

The representative informed Katie there were no flights available on their airline the next morning. Katie demanded a full refund. Surprisingly, the representative complied. She informed Katie that since our flight was changed and would require an overnight layover, we were entitled to a full refund. Why didn't she say so in the first place?

While listening to the conversation, I already knew our fate. I opened my wallet, pulled out my credit card, and researched flights before Katie finished her call. Feeling like a contestant on *The Amazing Race*, I searched for a new flight. Despite it nearing midnight, I wasn't deterred!

The Delta website showed a flight scheduled to depart Minneapolis at 6 a.m. It included a lengthy layover in Atlanta, but we would arrive at the Disney resort just in time for our dinner reservations. Only four of these golden tickets remained, and we quickly reserved two.

The maintenance guy wasn't too far off with his statement earlier that night. A trip to Walt Disney World IS expensive, and with the click of a button, the price increased by $900 for two one-way tickets.

We sat on our cushiony beds, quietly in a combined fog of disbelief and the overpowering aroma of bleach wafting up from the bedding, staring blankly at the bags of unopened food. It was twelve fifteen in the morning, and we had set our alarm clocks to ring in less than three hours to ensure we made it to the airport on time. Sleep deprivation would make for an interesting day.

After we boarded the completely full flight, we sighed in relief. We were tremendously thankful that we snagged two tickets only hours before departure. We were also grateful for the front desk preacher and her ramblings. Had it not been for her endless loop of, "I'm warning you's ..." and "You need to know's," our entire trip would likely have been ruined.

Though Katie and I frequently become trapped in annoying, nonsensical conversations with others, the time we spent in the ongoing sermon that night paid off. Now, whenever I purchase airline tickets with any airline, I hear the front desk preacher's words echo in my head, reminding me to check my flight status to ensure no changes have been made.

Though we initially found her over-explaining everything annoying, our lack of appropriate travel preparation had likely irritated her. But she probably encounters morons like us daily. Regardless, we will forever be thankful for the sermon that evening. In addition, her ongoing verbal antics helped us to become more patient, which we needed to deal with Orbitz, the undesirable airline, and with other travelers on only a few hours of sleep while en route to the most magical place on earth.

Oh, and, finally, "You need to know," the undesirable airline reimbursed our money in the end.

It's a Breeze

*I believe when life gives you lemons, you should make
lemonade ... and try to find someone whose life has
given them vodka and have a party.*

— *Ron White*

PURCHASING A NEW OR USED VEHICLE IS STRESSFUL, AT LEAST IN
our experience. It seems like there is always some obnoxious salesperson with no good intentions and a "we don't take no for an
answer" sales pitch roping us into our next piece of crap with its own
unique "problem package" included.

Our minivan was crumbling after our toddler drove backward
into a pole, making the rear door non-functional. The sliding side
door had a large dent from a deer ramming its head into it, and the
fan belt emitted a lengthy ear-piercing screech while the engine was
running.

My husband Paul and I headed to a local dealership and
requested to meet with Frank, a salesperson whom a friend highly
recommended. Frank was affable and not pushy. When he showed us

the lineup of new and used vehicles on the lot, it seemed like he genuinely cared about our needs.

A cranberry-red 1997 Plymouth Breeze caught our eye. There were two on the lot. Both had the same color, good aesthetic condition, and low mileage. However, one had a scratch inside the driver's door. Of course, we purchased the car without this imperfection. Finally, we had a flawless vehicle that we could rely on.

Little did we know we wouldn't even make it a year without issue. The vehicle that brought us excitement during the summer began its downturn that same winter. One frigid January day, we noticed a sizable pool of oil in our driveway, about twenty-four inches in circumference. This wasn't a good sign. We brought the car to the dealership's repair shop, where we purchased it, and they informed us that the problem was a broken oil seal.

The mechanic asked if the car had been in an accident, noting accidents can cause seals to break.

Frank was at work that day. We informed him of what was happening and the mechanic's question. He then logged into his computer to research the car's history.

"According to what I see, this vehicle has not been in any accidents." The mechanic replaced the oil seal for the low cost of $800 and sent us on our way.

Approximately a month later and continued frigid temperatures, another black puddle of fresh oil suddenly appeared in the driveway. We called the towing company, and they hauled the vehicle back to the shop. The mechanic informed us that yet another oil seal had busted. This pattern repeated multiple times that winter. The additional expense of the repairs was becoming overly burdensome on top of our already pricey monthly car payments.

We again spoke with Frank about this disaster, armed with the mother of all vehicle failure lingo, "LEMON LAW." However, we did not have our repair receipts, but we knew the repair shop had documentation of our frequent visits. Frank took us to speak with the shop manager to inquire further. After re-explaining our frustrations, the manager slithered into a back room to "check their records."

He came back and stated, "I'm sorry. We show no record of any repairs done on your car here at this shop."

"We've had our vehicle in this shop multiple times and have had multiple defective seals replaced." The shop manager refused to budge, maintaining they never fixed our car. Further discussion with Frank revealed we weren't eligible for the lemon law. We owed too much on our loan to afford to trade this vehicle in for a different one. We decided our best bet was to nurture that hunk of junk until we paid our loan in full.

The problems persisted. Each winter, when the temperatures hit subzero, seals failed. In December 1999, we trekked to Illinois to visit with my mom for our annual New Year's Eve celebration.

The temperature was brutal: minus double digits with the wind chill. As we backed up, we noticed a puddle of black gold in the driveway—the worst leak we had ever seen.

Paul drove to a gas station to check the oil. He pulled the dipstick out. There was no trace of oil on it. Our choices were to either have the car towed to a shop in Illinois or drive it back to central Wisconsin.

Paul purchased two twelve-quart cases of oil and dumped four quarts into the oil fill opening. We devised our "foolproof" plan, or what some might consider a fool's plan, to drive the broken beast back to Wisconsin. We roped my mom and aunt into following us in my mom's car just in case we broke down on the highway.

We squished a half dozen suitcases and dufflebags into the trunk and back seat of my mom's Grand Prix. Luckily, a little space was left in the back seat for Mike and Katie, our two youngest children, while my mom and aunt sat up front. This scene resembled an overloaded vehicle in a developing country minus the intense heat, sweaty bodies, and blown-out suspension struts and shocks. Paul, our oldest daughter Jackie, and I loaded into our piece of crap along with the cases of oil reserves needed for the nail-biting journey.

We proceeded on our way and drove thirty-seven and a half miles, at which point the bright-yellow oil light turned on. We stopped the car on the side of the road. Paul checked the oil stick. Sure enough, the engine was parched again. Obliging her thirst, he poured in another four quarts of black gold.

Throughout the entire trip, like clockwork, the little yellow light would shine brightly after we had driven exactly thirty-seven and a half miles. We'd pull onto the shoulder of the highway and roll to a stop.

Paul pulled the lever to release the hood latch and opened the driver's side door. A whoosh of unwelcome polar air forced its way into the car, quickly consuming any warmth within.

Jackie and I took turns standing beside Paul at each stop, holding a dim flashlight so he could locate the oil filler cap and position the container over the spout to pour in the required four quarts of petroleum. This process required the flashlight holder to remain as still as possible despite the uncontrollable shaking and shivering caused by the piercing bite of the cold air.

This game of stop-and-go, headlights cutting into the frigid night, filling the engine with crude lifeblood, went on for 230.3 miles. That night, we burned twenty-four quarts of oil. Luckily, this process effectively got us home by the twenty-fourth hour, just in time to ring in the new year.

The following day, Paul went outside to discover that our cranberry-red car had transformed into jet black. Traveling sixty-five miles per hour while spewing crude oil caused this fantastic transformation. We had our own model of the Exxon Valdez disaster but on wheels. The tow truck soon picked up our environmental hazard, hauling it to a repair shop. The main rear oil seal and head gaskets were the most recent parts to blow under the icy, cold Midwestern temperatures.

We finally paid off our loan after what felt like a lifetime of payments. The towing guy hoisted the clunk of crap onto a flatbed and hauled it off to a junkyard, but the oil stain in the middle of our driveway remained as a constant reminder that it is not a breeze owning a Breeze.

A couple of years later, we happened upon a *Consumer Reports* magazine. For kicks and giggles, we reviewed the ratings and found that of all the Breezes made, our year/model of Plymouth Breeze had the worst ratings. The issues were failing oil seals and head gaskets.

Though not the only victims, we were likely the bravest and most adventurous of all Breeze owners. Our last-minute decision to purchase stock in the petroleum industry and embark on a family road trip on a frigid New Year's Eve was certainly a recipe for disaster. Still, we prevailed. Our family proved to be a well-oiled machine that functioned better than the actual well-oiled machine we traveled in that evening.

Uninvited Attention

Insecure people seek attention. Confident people are given attention without even trying.

— *Ziad K. Abdelnour*

Those closest to me have an overload of opportunities to hear tales of craziness and experience my unique talents. It's a daily comedy extravaganza of storytelling and performances. "America's Got Talent," look out! I do impersonations, demonstrate dance moves crazier than Elaine in *Seinfeld*, and throw in an occasional juggling act.

Being silly, fun, and zany is my jive. However, I do not reveal my extrovert-ish tendencies when I meet a new person. Why? Because I am introvert-ish—quiet and reserved until I get to know you. Obviously, the "Stranger Danger" child safety chant of the past certainly did a number on my brain.

However, despite my efforts to stay under the radar, life occasionally has a different plan, creating scenarios that draw uninvited attention.

The Ultimate Advertisement

 We love to see you smile.

— McDonald's Slogan, early 2000s

SOME PEOPLE ARE EXHIBITIONIST EXTRAORDINAIRES. THESE folks enjoy putting themselves out there, being noticed, determined to be the center of attention. My husband is quite the opposite. He cringes at the thought of being the focal point and avoids it at all costs. His discomfort includes giving speeches, doing television interviews, engaging in TED Talks, singing and/or dancing. Basically, any activity that involves an actual or imaginary stage. However, once Paul broke out of his shell and began a unique advertising campaign.

One spring morning, Paul and I were headed to the Cultural Festival, an annual family event held at our town's local high school. This immersive experience allowed area residents to enjoy multicultural costumes and dances, beautifully handmade arts and crafts, and unique cuisines.

Despite the variety of food options awaiting us at the event, our stomachs were grumbling loud, indicating that we could not wait. We pulled into the local McDonald's drive-thru.

A chipper voice belted from the speaker. "Welcome to McDonald's. May I take your order?"

"Yes, I'll take an Egg McMuffin, a sausage burrito with hot sauce, and two large unsweetened iced teas."

After paying for and picking up our bag of unhealthy choices, we devoured our meal within minutes before arriving at the festival.

After paying our entrance fee, we strolled side by side for a couple of hours. First, we perused the commons area and first-floor hallways, stopping at more than a dozen ethnic vendor booths and observing the artisans as they created and sold their lovely handmade crafts, baked goods, and wares. We made it a point to mingle with each one, learning about their unique cultures and crafting processes. Some vendors taught crafting to youngsters. This made us smile as we reminisced about a time when our kids used to participate in these annual activities.

The sounds of traditional multiethnic instruments and beats filtered down the long hallway, drawing eager attendees toward the gymnasium. The blended symphony of aromas of ethnic cuisine filled the air. We made our way through the sea of people and walked through the doorway. Food vendors spanned the perimeter of the gymnasium, additional artisans lined rows in the center, while singers and dancers in colorful costumes entertained the audience from the stage at the opposite end of the room.

Each year, this popular event drew a few hundred or more residents, local news, and radio stations, so we were always guaranteed to run into several of our friends. We had reached the pinnacle of our sensory overload breaking point after two hours of pushing through crowds, snacking on greasy jerk chicken, and trying to talk above the blaring music. We headed to our vehicle.

As we were putting our seatbelts on, Paul noticed something peculiar stuck to the crotch area of his jeans. It was the round, white sticker about the size of a silver dollar used to seal the end of his breakfast burrito wrapper.

The sticker didn't have the signature Golden Arches logo on it to indicate that it came off a McDonald's product. Rather, printed in big bold letters, it said "SAUSAGE."

We busted out in uncontrollable roaring laughter. *How did we not notice this sticker stuck to his pants?* McDonalds has a familiar advertising campaign, but the fact that their food packaging turned into an entirely different form of advertising was even more classic than the Big Mac sandwich itself! There wasn't even a slight chance that this clear marketing message could have been missed by fellow fair goers, and it is likely that those who witnessed this innocent publicity stunt thought, "What a freaking weirdo!" Move over Ronald, Grimace, and Hamburglar! McRamsey was the new kid in town!

From time to time, we find ourselves at a McDonalds drive-thru. On occasion, Paul orders a breakfast burrito, and we find ourselves giggling when we see the familiar white sticker with reddish-brown lettering. However, after the laughter has subsided and we arrive at our destination, Paul always makes sure to check his pants before heading in.

The Naughty List!

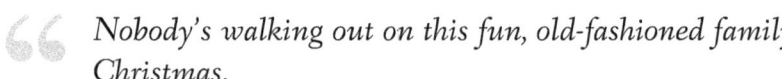

Nobody's walking out on this fun, old-fashioned family Christmas.

— *Christmas Vacation*, 1989

EACH PERSON HAS THEIR OWN WAY OF CELEBRATING OR NOT celebrating the holidays. I am personally a Thanksgiving diehard due to the simplicity and lack of commercialism and because it includes overdoses of sleep-inducing tryptophan. On the other hand, my daughter Katie is a traditionalist. She loves all holidays, but Christmas is one of her all-time favorites.

Although I enjoy some parts of Christmas, such as meals with the family, festive holiday decorations, and classic Christmas movies. What I dread most about this holiday is the added stress of gift buying, wrapping, decorating, being the peacekeeper, and ensuring everyone is happy and enjoying themselves. Oddly, the list of downfalls associated with Christmas is highlighted in many of the beloved Christmas movies I tend to gravitate to. These storylines of absolute holiday chaos with overarching themes of the "true meaning of

Christmas" are relatable to many and likely contribute to folks giving Christmas another try year after year.

In January 2021, I decided enough was enough. Our kids were grown, our family could do a *Christmas with the Kranks*. If you haven't seen this film, the storyline goes like this: Mr. and Mrs. Krank's adult daughter Blair leaves the country for a job with the Peace Corps. Since Christmas "won't be the same" without their daughter home, they decide to skip Christmas altogether and book a cruise vacation. (On a side note, I love this movie. It's full of *Burnt Gloveboxes* adventures.)

Though the concept flopped in the movie, I thought we could successfully pull it off. I presented the idea of going to the Florida Keys during the first week in December in lieu of our regular Christmas celebration, and EVERYONE in the family agreed with this plan.

We planned our trip, and things were on track until October rolled around, and the guilt trip began.

"We are at least going to do stockings, right, Mom?" Katie asked.

"No, remember, the Keys trip is instead of Christmas."

"But our stockings are tradition, Mom! It won't be the same without them. Please ..."

Did I mention that Katie is an adult? However, her youthful spirit takes over when it comes to holidays, and traditional values and practices trump sensibility and practicality.

Feeling guilty about the possibility of breaking her heart, I surrendered against my better judgment. Since I had already planned to put up the tree so I could enjoy the festive lights, I felt she could at least have her stockings. Also, much of this final decision was self-preservation on my part. She would make me pay for the rest of my life via constant reminders of how I selfishly ruined our holiday had I not complied.

I happened to be out with my best friend, and I informed her about our original plan for an all-out Christmas boycott, which had suddenly morphed, the stockings making their way in.

A woman overheard the story and said, "Yeah, I tried doing a *Christmas with the Kranks* one year, and it did not work out well."

Despite this woman's inability to carry out the boycotting Christmas plan, I was determined to be successful, aside from the stockings and the lit tree!

Well, you know the phrase, "Give an inch, and they take a mile?" I am convinced some fortune teller saw our scenario unfold in her crystal ball.

Our son, Mike, approached me with a photo on his cell phone and said, "Mom, this is what I REALLY want for Christmas this year."

When I reminded him of our original plan, he said, "FINE! THEN I'LL BUY MY OWN PRESENTS THIS YEAR!"

His protest of my boycott inevitably led to our annual name exchange, during which we each purchased a sixty dollar gift for our recipient.

To avoid battling the holiday crowds, I ordered many of my gifts online and, therefore, depended on companies to deliver them unharmed to my home. However, my goal did not coincide with the delivery services.

One gift had a label that read, "Handle with love. Do not bend."

In the corner where that label read loud and clear, the protective cardboard was ripped off the package, and the corner was significantly bent. In an attempt to report the issue to the shipping company, I received the message, "This shipment is not eligible for reporting unsatisfactory shipping."

What does that mean? The only reason for reporting is for the purpose of notifying the company something is unsatisfactory, whether it be shipping, product damage, or, in this case, both were applicable.

The second package I received was marked FRAGILE (pronounced, of course, *fra-gee-lay* in homage to *A Christmas Story*). I believe this word is Italian for "drop-kick this item as hard as you can from the street to the landing of the porch."

Apparently, the delivery person knew how to read and translate

Italian well and had also been a kicker for an NFL team at some point. The box had a huge dent in the corner, just shy of the actual tread pattern from the delivery person's shoe. Surprisingly, the gift was not broken, but had it been, it was likely ineligible for unsatisfactory shipping.

Next, I also ordered a book for my son-in-law. When the package arrived, I opened it. Instead of a new book with the aroma of freshly printed crisp pages, I found a used library book with yellowed pages, the library name stamped in red inside the front cover, and a little slot inside the back cover for the checkout card. On the positive side, another tree wasn't killed to produce a new finished product.

The doozy of a finale to this Christmas season occurred during my work Christmas Party! A couple of years earlier, I purchased an adorable Christmas sweater on sale for six dollars. The design included a tropical scene with two palm trees, a hammock slung between them, and Santa Claus lounging in it. The print read, "Let it snow, let it snow, let it snow." This Christmas sweater, though far from ugly, was meant for me. I received so many compliments and took great pride in my nifty bargain purchase.

Since I'd had the sweater for several Christmases, I thought it was probably time to wash it. I turned the sweater inside out, used the gentlest wash cycles, and carefully hung it to air dry. Our work Christmas Party was held virtually via Teams. I wore my newly laundered festive sweater. Once the party ended, I went to the bathroom.

I glanced in the mirror while washing my hands. *Oh no!* Somehow, the agitating and spinning had washed off Santa's iconic red suit. Jolly ol' Saint Nick now lay in the hammock wearing only a hat, boots, white wrist cuffs, and a teeny tiny piece of the white trim from his coat draped across his groin area. It looked like he was sporting a pair of Fruit of the Loom tighty whities. Santa's "little package" was on display.

I burst into uncontrollable laughter. My cheek muscles burned, torso muscles strained, and tears poured down my face while the

"What the craps" spewed from my mouth in between the gasps of air and outbursts of snorts and chuckles.

This naked Santa sprawled out in all his glory in a tropical paradise was a product quality malfunction to the highest degree. The paint was either accidentally defective or a disgruntled factory worker deliberately used wash-off paint on my Santa to undermine the company after being denied his holiday leave.

My once adorable Christmas sweater had fully transformed into the most hideous of all ugly Christmas sweaters, featuring Saint Nicholas in his birthday suit. It would surely win any Ugly Christmas Sweater Contest.

Bathroom Bully

 Life is like toilet paper. You're either on a roll or taking crap from someone.

— *Unknown*

SEVERAL INTERNET MEMES SAY, *"BATHROOM BREAK, THEY WILL find you."* The meme is from the perspective of the person inside the bathroom and shows the bottom of a bathroom door where it meets the floor. The tiny hand of a child or a cat's paw reaches under the door's crack. No meme is as accurate as this. You need a couple of minutes of alone time to take care of business in privacy. It never fails that someone or something pounds or scratches on the door while crying, meowing, barking, or whining.

Public restrooms seem to eliminate (no pun intended) the problem of interruptions altogether. Don't get me wrong; there have been a few occasions in public restrooms where a small child crawls on the disgusting floor under the stall, the mother scolding the child, "Get back over here!"

There have also been a handful of times in which I have chosen the stall with the wacky lock that doesn't work, and someone comes busting in, unaware that I am there in all my glory. Immediately turning red, the person quickly retreats, stating, "Sorry!" and then heads to the nearest hole in the wall and crawls in.

However, other than those rare unpleasant occurrences, public restrooms seem to be a place of peace to take care of business with minimal interruptions.

One night, Paul and I met up with a couple of friends at a local bar/restaurant right up the road from us. This place was famous for its delicious food and reasonable prices. We had a great time with our friends, eating and socializing. I told Paul I needed to use the facilities as we prepared to leave for home.

I strolled into the ladies' room and chose the first of the two stalls. After I closed the door, I heard someone enter the restroom. She made her way into the stall next to me. Then, the woman began talking.

"Hi. How are you doing?"

Then a moment of silence.

"Can you hear me? Hello ...?"

Another moment of silence.

"Fine, don't talk to me!"

The whole time I listened, I thought this woman was talking on her phone. It reminded me of when my mom, who was close to retirement, called me from her work bathroom to tell me she missed me. Even though I thought the timing odd, I was quite proud of my mom, who was a stickler for following the rules, even the unwritten ones. (Thanks, Mom, for passing that trait on to me!)

This memory made me smile, and I started wondering who this lady was calling. *Was she calling a secret lover? Or was she calling her beloved daughter from the stall?*

The woman seemed irritated with whomever this person was because their responses didn't meet her expectations. Or maybe she had a poor phone connection. She fell silent. I left my stall, hoping to wash my hands and leave to allow her privacy to continue with whatever shenanigans she was engaging in.

As I dried my hands, the other stall door swung open, revealing a woman about five feet tall, her hair pulled up into a messy bun, and she was sporting an ordinary T-shirt and jeans.

She charged toward me and said, "Hi, my name is Jenny. Do you not answer when someone is talking to you?"

She stood within inches of me, glaring, waiting for an answer. Gut tightened and heart racing, I stuttered, "I-I'm sorry. I didn't know you were talking to me. I thought you were on the phone."

"Why would you think I was talking on the phone? I was talking to you!"

I stood there staring at her, shaking my head. I'm confident my mouth hung open, making me look like a character in a Saturday morning cartoon. I pivoted and scurried out, leaving my newfound "friend" standing there.

Still fearing the wrath of Jenny, I felt we needed to leave before she approached me again. My husband and our friends continued to talk and laugh, having a grand ol' time. I sat there, quietly in disbelief over what had transpired. The phrase "What goes on behind closed doors" takes on a whole new meaning when bathroom stall doors are involved.

I watched Jenny leave the bathroom; she didn't make eye contact with me as she staggered back to the bar, obviously drunk or on something. While the conversation at our table continued, I periodically glanced over at the bar, keeping tabs on Jenny. At one point, I lost sight of her. My anxiety grew worse as I did not know where she had disappeared to. My heart pounding again, I quickly scanned my surroundings. *Where did she go? Is she outside waiting to pounce on me?*

There was no sign of her anywhere when we left the restaurant. We made our way to our car, my eyes darting around on the lookout. Paul unlocked the door; I hopped in and breathed a deep sigh of relief when I shut the door.

During our ride home, Paul asked, "Is everything okay? You became so quiet at the table."

"I was bullied in the bathroom!" I told him about the scene that played out and how thankful I was to have survived the ordeal.

"I saw that lady! She was over at the bar. She looked extremely intoxicated. I saw her swaying and stumbling around." Paul said.

Of course, he saw her! Paul is always fully aware of his surroundings. Unfortunately, he hadn't honed in his ESP skills to let me know I should have avoided using the restroom that evening.

As usual, he didn't seem too shocked by this tale of craziness. He simply said, "Only you, Gina."

Even now, I ponder Jenny's intentions. I'll never know if she sought a friend or a fight. After that night, I never saw her again. When the anxiety from my encounter with the bathroom bully lifted, I could look back on the isolated incident, shake my head, and giggle. This was the most bizarre experience I have ever had in a public restroom, and it certainly gave me a greater appreciation for little fingers or paws reaching under the crack of the door during my bathroom breaks at home.

Too Close for Comfort

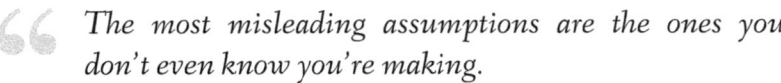 *The most misleading assumptions are the ones you
don't even know you're making.*

— *Douglas Adams*

THE COVID-19 PANDEMIC WAS QUITE THE RIDE FOR EVERYONE,
bringing considerable controversy and polarization globally.
However, many people can agree on one thing: the pandemic
brought about monumental craziness many of us will never forget.
Many of us wouldn't have made it if we didn't find some form of
humor during this madness.

The absurdity began in March 2020, when grocery stores were
ransacked. Certain items became hot commodities for reasons we will
never know. Toilet paper, hand soap, pizza, and diapers were among
the favorites of panicked, pandemic-stricken shoppers. Shelves that
once held these items were bare as if the supply trucks had stopped
providing shipments altogether.

The next wave of craziness was the surge of innovation. Photos of creative shoppers sporting unique face and body coverings were splattered all over the media to avoid all possible contact with the virus. Military gas masks, unicorn and dinosaur costume heads, and hazmat suits provided a sense of security during lengthy outings for shoppers in search of more packages of toilet paper.

Fast forward to 2022, many communities had lifted masking mandates in public venues. Since restrictions were lifted in our town, Paul and .I discontinued masking where it was not required. However, we remained respectful to individuals who continued to don the facial fabric. Raging controversy and division continued, and for our own self-preservation, we avoided all masking debates.

Though hoarding toilet paper and debating masking protocol were the typical activities during the pandemic, WE opted to begin gambling and started a small business. The previous owner had neglected the space we were renting. It was filthy and required extensive cleanup, causing dust and dirt particles to become airborne.

With each inhalation, my lungs felt heavy, as if I were an avid chain smoker. Since coughing and wheezing remained socially unacceptable, we had no choice but to resort back to masking, at least during the cleanup.

We drove to Menards, a local big-box hardware store, to pick up additional cleaning solvents, supplies, and masks. As usual, we wasted time aimlessly wandering up one aisle and down another, gazing at items we didn't need for the project at hand. Eventually, we made our way to the cleaning supplies we needed and filled our cart.

As we headed to the register, Paul stopped abruptly and said, "We forgot the masks! Stay here with the cart. I'll run back to get them."

"While you do that, I'm going over to the Christmas aisle. Meet me there when you are done." I responded.

He agreed.

Christmas had passed, which meant holiday items were on sale. This was an excellent opportunity to uphold my knack for financial irresponsibility by purchasing stuff I didn't need. I was totally sucked back into the Christmas spirit, captivated by all the colorful decorations, and losing track of time.

Suddenly, I heard Paul's voice from across the aisle. "There you are!"

He quickly made his way over to me. He leaned in and quietly said, "I just had an odd encounter with a woman. She was the same height as you, had the same color hair, and was wearing a long, dark blue coat, just like yours. Seeing her from a distance, I thought it was you. I walked right up to her, slid in close like this ...." Demonstrating, he moved up next to me, pressing his left shoulder into my right. "I was looking down at the box of masks when I did this, so still did not notice it wasn't you. Then I said, 'I picked out just the right kind of masks for you.' I heard her gasp, and I quickly looked up. Not only was she NOT you, but she also wasn't wearing a mask. I quickly stepped away from her."

He said initially, the woman just stood there, frozen, her mouth hanging open, as if insulted by the audacity of this stranger telling her what type of mask he selected for her, much less the suggestion she should be wearing a mask in the first place.

Paul continued, "Then she asked me, 'Do I know you?' I said, 'I'm so sorry; I thought you were my wife.'" He said the woman reluctantly accepted his apology and quickly left the Christmas aisle and headed toward the registers.

Paul is usually in tune with his surroundings, having the visual acuity of a hawk. On the other hand, I have extremely poor awareness in public settings. Paul has repeatedly preached to me about the importance of maintaining social awareness. Obviously, his long-winded but well-intended lectures have yet to sink in, given my double was nearby in the Menards Christmas section, and I had no clue.

That day, Paul lost all focus. He became so excited about buying masks that he uncharacteristically approached a perfect stranger during a global pandemic, social distancing out the window, and brought up this controversial topic of suggesting the type of mask to wear.

In the end, I'm glad he survived that interesting interaction. Whatever side of the spectrum you fall on regarding this contentious subject, there is no masking the irony of Paul's untimely and awkward interaction with the stranger that day.

I'm Not Worthington

 I miss being able to slam my phone down when I hang up on someone. Violently pressing "End Call" doesn't do it for me.

— Unknown

TECHNOLOGY NEVER CEASES TO AMAZE ME. SCIENTISTS successfully send spacecraft on explorative missions to Mars. They maneuver these robotic machines from a building on the east coast of Florida to collect photos, scientific samples, and data. However, we've yet to solve cell phone tower transmission issues on Earth.

When I moved to Superior, Wisconsin, my calls dropped into the abyss. A representative from my cell phone carrier informed me they did not have towers in this area, causing my calls to drop. The rep suggested that I change cell providers.

The doorbell chimed softly as I walked through the glass door at the local Verizon store, notifying the two representatives that another sucker had sauntered in. One smiled at me and said, "Someone will be right with you." I nodded, and both continued to present their confusing sales pitches to perplexed customers.

The store's ambiance drew me in like a bug heading toward the light of death. Walls decorated with colorful protective cases surrounded me, and accessories hung in well-organized, horizontal rows. The overhead lighting beamed down, illuminating the merchandise below. White pedestals showcased the latest and most expensive iPhone and Samsung Galaxy models in the store, enticing impulsive consumers with enhanced photographs of colorful scenes. These well-designed corporate displays weaken the willpower of even the tightest miser.

Eventually, the representative and I sat down at the desk of doom. In front of me was a box with a shiny $1,200 Android nestled inside. The representative handed me a tablet with a list of phone number options to choose from. The last four digits of one sequence were 2570, nearly the same last digits of my childhood phone number. Winner, winner, chicken dinner!

Of course, when cell phone carriers give you a "new number," it's not usually new at all. Relying on nostalgia mnemonics to select my new number added an ongoing *Burnt Glovebox* story to my repertoire. My phone number previously belonged to a person with one name, alias "Worthington."

Mononyms are not limited to celebrities like Madonna, Prince, or Elvis. People often have nicknames or pet names. For example, those closest to me have called me "Bean" for years, and the nickname stuck. Even my grandson refers to me as Grandma Bean.

Though I love my nickname, I do not use it everywhere. I'm certain most United States citizens use their legal names, especially when interacting in professional settings. However, this was not the case for Worthington.

One day, my phone rang. The number was unrecognizable, so I allowed the call to route directly to my voicemail.

The message said, "Hey, Worthington, this is Joe from Moving It

Trucking Company. We have a load for you. If you would like it, give us a call and let us know."

Must have the wrong number. I deleted the message and went on with my day.

With increasing frequency, I received messages from trucking companies located all over the United States. One day, I received a voicemail from a Texas trucking company informing Worthington that a load was ready to be picked up. Feeling spicy, I returned the call. I informed the company that the phone number no longer belonged to Worthington. Apparently, I inadvertently became Worthington's personal secretary.

"Sorry, ma'am," the woman on the other end said in her Texan drawl. "Do you have Worthington's new number?"

"No, I don't even know who Worthington is," I snapped, irritated.

"Well, we will surely remove this number from our system. Thank you. Y'all have a nice day now."

Years into this fiasco, I stopped at Walgreens for some items and a prescription. The cashier asked me if I was a member of the Walgreens Rewards Program. I confirmed but could not remember which phone number I had used to enroll.

The cashier said, "Well, let's try one number; if that doesn't work, we can try the other number."

I offered the number ending in 2570. She quickly typed it into the register, looked up briskly, and stated, "Worthington?"

I felt shocked, amused, and irritated all at once. Seriously? Giggling at the insanity of the ongoing scenario, I told the cashier, "No, I am not Worthington!"

I shared with her the story of my now less-than-desirable phone number. She stood staring blankly at me with a flat affect as I rambled through the lengthy tale of the Worthington woes.

Since 2013, the calls have expanded to other entities. The most interesting was a message I received from Lowe's informing Worthington that his lumber order had arrived. *Worthington recently ordered lumber but did not inform Lowe's of the correct contact information?*

Despite where the calls have originated, one thing has remained consistent: they all ask for the one, the only, "Worthington."

Considering the chain of events, would it be wildly unreasonable to consider the possibility that I could receive a text message for Worthington while writing this story? Absolutely not! Within a half hour of writing, I received a text message. It read:

> Good morning! This is Doug at U R Trucking. I was seeing if you had an end dump available Thursday or Friday for a load of Roofing Granules coming out of Merrill, WI, going to Dayton, OH. Several loads. Paying 124/TON. If you'd wanna help with this, then please let me know. Thanks in advance!

Doug did not expressly state that he intended this text for Worthington. However, it is more probable than not, as I have never received a non-Worthington hauling request from a trucking company.

The twists and turns I have been through as Worthington's personal assistant have certainly brought a whole new level of amusement to my already interesting life and an additional chuckle to many of my days. Though I sometimes wonder, *What makes ME so special and deserving to have so many unique experiences, including one involving this man of mystery? Am I truly worthy enough?*

The answer is clear, "Yes, I am worthy! BUT ... I AM NOT WORTHINGTON!"

Critters Gone Wild

Nope, nope, nope!

— *Gina Ramsey*

I do not like anything that creeps, crawls, pinches, stings, flies, or lurks in the night. Though certain mammals, reptiles, and crustaceans give me the heebie-jeebies when they get a little too close for comfort, the world of insects, arthropods, arachnids, and flying mammals put me over the edge.

These are monstrosities in disguise, many carrying a powerful punch of venom-induced discomfort or severe illness with one bite, pinch, or sting. Whether they have six, eight, one hundred, or one thousand legs, I hyperventilate anytime one of these vile creatures comes anywhere near my personal bubble.

There are YouTube videos and even horror movies that demonstrate the ways people handle encounters with these beasts. Techniques used include running, screaming, flailing arms (hands open or closed fists), stomping, or spraying Aqua Net, otherwise known as a liquid helmet, to bring undesirable creepy crawlies to their demise.

Becoming an expert in all these approaches is mandatory for survival when a "NOPE!" attack is looming.

Some refer to insects as "harmless," saying, "Well, if you leave them alone, they will leave you alone." Not true! Once, I was walking outside minding my own business, and a yellow jacket stung me on the ankle without being provoked, thus proving they all have a vendetta against me. My main goal is to remain as far away from all creepy-crawly creatures as possible. However, these hooligans always find time in their day to torment me.

The Punishment

 *You must pay for your sins. If you have already paid,
please ignore this notice.*

— *Sam Levenson*

AMY, VALERIE, AND I WORKED TOGETHER AT THE WOMEN'S
Community, an agency that provided safety and advocacy for individuals affected by domestic and sexual violence. This was grueling
work. The traumatic stories we heard daily could not be unheard.
Many of us experienced symptoms of vicarious trauma as a result of
stepping into the trenches.

Conferences allowed us the opportunity to *sharpen the saw*—
learn the newest information in our profession, and also offered a
needed break. One particular conference offered learning opportunities far beyond the keynote speaker and breakout sessions. This
conference was held at the Kalahari Resort in Wisconsin Dells, a city
in Wisconsin coined "the waterpark capital of the world." A few of us
thought it would be fun to check out the Ho-Chunk Casino after our
daylong training. Amy decided to hang back at the hotel for dinner

and relaxation, so it was down to Valerie, me, and two nurses we knew, Erin and Donna.

Erin insisted on driving. Her car was tiny, just shy of what you'd see driving under the big top at a circus. Valerie and I felt like Ringling Brothers clowns as we squished tightly into the back seat. The two nurses sat up front.

None of us knew the casino's location, so we stopped at a gas station on the corner of the intersection near our hotel to ask for directions. We drove slowly, perpendicular to the busy gas pumps, carefully scanning. We spotted a woman wearing a long plain dress; her dishwater blonde hair was gathered into one braid draped down her back, looking like a modern-day character from *Little House on the Prairie*. She was pumping fuel into her full-size cargo van. Assuming she was a local, we decided to ask her for directions.

Donna rolled down her window and yelled, "Excuse me, can you tell us how to get to the Ho-Chunk Casino?"

The woman responded with an overzealous willingness to give instructions, "Sure! Drive up to the light and make a left. Merge onto the highway and head south. That should take you right to the casino."

Donna yelled back, "Thank you so much," while the rest of us repeated the directions a few times to ensure a step was not missed.

With a cunning smile and snark in her voice, she said, "You are *sooo* welcome," almost as if she was mocking us.

After this confident but weird response, we all joked that she was probably involved in some religion whose teachings prohibit gambling of any kind. In an attempt to teach us a good lesson, she deliberately sent us on a wild goose chase, leading us heathens far from the house of sin. Figuring that was a silly theory, we trustingly followed her instructions.

Traveling on the highway at sixty-five miles per hour, no exits could be found in the darkness. Our theory about being punished grew more probable. We hoped that we would see the casino at some point.

Suddenly, I noticed a giant June bug on the window beside Valerie and began screaming in pure horror. Valerie followed suit. She whipped her seat belt off in a split second and jumped onto my lap, providing extra security for me and protecting me from the vile creature lurking inside the vehicle. My hands gripped her upper arms to keep her in that spot.

In a panic, I yelled out to Erin, "Roll down the window!" hoping the disgusting critter would get sucked out, but suddenly realized the mighty wind would likely lift that bug and fling it in our direction.

Quickly retracting my previous statement, I began yelling, "No, roll the window back up! Roll it up!"

Given the urgency, the window went back up at what felt like a snail's pace. I saw the bug drop to the floor. In a panic, I begged Erin to stop the car while she attempted to convince us that this little bug would not hurt us. Our beetle-infested clown mobile continued to move at supersonic speed into the night.

Silence fell, like that moment in a horror film, right before the killer jumped out to make his final slashing. Hearts beating, shallow breathing, knowing it was lurking in the darkness.

Valerie released herself from my death grip and slowly returned to her seat. Her knees were up, feet hovering as if in a half-fetal position, but this position did her no good, as the bug had made its way to the back window on her side. Throats already raw, we began screaming, horrified to see the fiend resurface. Valerie's seat belt flew off once again, and she launched herself back onto my lap.

I yelled toward Erin, pleading with her, "Please, Erin, stop the car, please! I'm begging you. This thing is going to kill us!"

She laughed hysterically.

In a shaky voice, I asked, "What is so funny? This thing is going to kill us!"

"I'm not bothered by bugs," she continued to laugh at our supposed exaggerated response. Our desperate cries for help, though real and warranted in our opinion, continued to fall on deaf ears. In

Erin's defense, the deafness was likely due to our screaming, but that was beside the point.

The creature disappeared again. Terrified, Valerie and I waited, listened, and carefully looked around, adrenaline surging through our veins, hearts pounding. Suddenly, a piercing shriek came from the front passenger seat. Donna's arms began flailing, and Valerie and I joined her in unison.

The oversized beetle had flown to the front of the vehicle and grazed the top of Donna's head midflight. Still screaming, Donna pulled the hood of her sweatshirt over her head and pulled the draw-strings so tight that only her nose could be seen.

I shoved Valerie off my lap, threw the top half of my body onto the center console armrest, and screamed out like Chris Farley, "For the love of God, stop the car!"

Erin finally pulled the car over to the shoulder, and we all jumped out into the tall weeds, still screaming but laughing simultaneously. I just about peed myself from the combination of terror and laughter deriving from the knowledge that the hard-shelled creature was still in the car while imagining what more could be lurking in the overgrown roadside plant life we now found ourselves standing in.

We stood in utter blackness, dumbfounded at the distance we had traveled with no sight of an exit, much less a casino. Periodic headlights from oncoming cars shined on us, Erin and Donna did a blind scan of the clown car but did not find the critter. We figured perhaps it escaped the car when the doors opened. Having no choice, we squished back into the circus mobile and continued to drive, still attempting to find an exit.

At that point, we were all sure the lady at the gas pump had cursed us.

Could she have deliberately led us on this path away from the casino while also summoning the bug from the underworld to make us pay for our corruption, our wickedness?

Finally, an exit with a brightly lit gas station appeared. We pulled in and exited the car. As we stood there with the doors wide open, the giant beetle flew out and up to the bright lights above. Unbeknownst to us, the ghastly behemoth still lurked in the car during that final stretch to the gas station.

Erin asked a woman who had stopped for gas, "Do you know where the Ho-Chunk Casino is located?"

She informed us, "The casino is located back in Baraboo. I am heading in that direction. You can follow me if you'd like."

We followed her for approximately thirty minutes and finally arrived at the casino. The entire journey took us approximately an hour and fifteen minutes.

We headed in and strolled around in the thick, cigarette-smoke-filled air just long enough to get a dose of stimulation overload from the bright lights, repetitive chimes, and jangly music omitted from the hundreds of slot machines.

We were done and, quite frankly, exhausted from the energy spent on the lengthy battle with the creature from the underworld. We asked the casino security guard if he could give us directions to the Kalahari Resort, further explaining our extensive pilgrimage to the Ho-Chunk Casino. Shocked by our story, he informed us our resort was only one mile down the road.

During the one-mile trek back to the resort, we were at a loss for words, though we had a lot to say. We just experienced a one-hour drive from hell in a clown car, hard-shelled spawn of Hades in tow, while our destination was only one mile away? The GPS in the long dress had achieved her goal of making us repent of our transgressions, but not without a fight.

Long story short, we were too tired to gamble after the battle with the beast and the long drive. On a positive note, we saved a lot of money that evening.

The Maine Issue

 Trees ... they're all bark and no bite.

— Anonymous

It was a cool and foggy autumn morning in Bar Harbor, Maine. I stood near the start line with my husband Paul, my friend Kelly, her husband Rob, and about 200 others, getting ready to run the Mount Desert Island Half Marathon. Rob and I would run 13.1 miles that day while Kelly and Paul would be at the finish line to cheer us on.

As I listened to the commentator give the race details and encouragement to all the racers, I decided to do a little warm-up. As I stretched, I felt a twinge in my back between the shoulder blades. With every breath, the pain widened, covering the entire region of my upper back to the point in which my respiration was reduced to careful, shallow breaths.

I was in a slight panic. I needed my lungs to expand and contract freely from the start line until the end of the race. I asked Paul to massage my back, but his efforts were in vain. Every breath was agonizing. I kept trying to relax and take calming breaths, to no avail.

When this issue happened in the past, I put the corner edge of a wall directly between my shoulder blades and applied pressure along the strained area. Urgently, I quickly analyzed my surroundings. As you might expect, there are no walls in the outdoor landscape of Bar Harbor. But there were trees, many trees!

I felt desperate enough to see if a tree could provide the same measure of relief, so I leaned my spine against a trunk and attempted to roll the problem area against it. It didn't work.

I decided to give this roll technique another try and went to a second tree. Spine to the trunk, rolling left to right, I attempted to really dig the tree trunk into the area of discomfort. Neither tree massage had improved my pain, and each breath continued to be excruciating. Anxious, I knew I would have to deal with this issue throughout the race.

Rob and I walked to the start line. The air horn blew, and we were off. Initially, I felt the radiating, stabbing pain wrapping across my back as if it were trying to suffocate me. I continued to breathe through the discomfort. Then, the iliotibial band on my outer right knee flared up. The ache radiated upward along my outer thigh. As the pain in my leg increased, the back pain dissipated. I continued limping my way, mile by mile.

My feet pounded the pavement repetitively, and the stunning scenery took me aback. The road wound through the fog. Towering trees outstretched their branches high above the road. Colorful autumn leaves of reds, oranges, and yellows floated down, softly connecting with the earth.

The saltwater bay, fed by the mighty Atlantic Ocean, wrapped along the left side of the winding roadway. Lobster trap buoys and fishing boats dotted the water. With each meditative inhalation and exhalation of the crisp, salty air, I was thankful that my back pain had eased and for the opportunity to run through this picturesque landscape.

At about mile four, I decided to make a quick pit stop at the port-a-potties. While inside, I quickly and strategically began to adjust my race clothing and gear so that I could get my business done.

Back on my trek, I immediately felt an itchy, stinging sensation all over my back from my mid-waist up.

I thought, *Is my skin chaffing? What an odd place for this to happen, as my shirt cannot be rubbing that much on this area of my back."*

Continuing to run along, the sensation eventually went away, likely because the knee discomfort started up again.

It began drizzling midrace, making the fall air much chillier. I pushed through, hobbling to the finish line, where Paul, Rob, and Kelly patiently waited. After grabbing my well-earned commemorative medal and banana, we soon returned to our rental home to shower and power up for an afternoon of sightseeing.

In preparation for my shower, I removed my race shirt, and what I saw in the mirror was a sight to behold. My entire back and side had a dozen or more quarter-sized welts. This was what I felt when I exited the port-a-potty. Something bit me, and from the looks of it, there was more than one culprit who caused this type of destruction to the skin on my torso.

After my shower, I showed the bites to Paul and our friends, and they were shocked at how badly I had been eaten up. I became a half marathon chew toy for some critter. The bites were itchier and more painful than mosquito bites. It felt as if needles were continuously poking into my skin, and this sensation worsened with any form of physical activity, including walking.

I did an extensive Google search because, of course, that's the best place to find accurate information. Nonetheless, though I am not one hundred percent positive, I am certain CHIGGERS attacked me. From what I read, those buggers like to hang out on the trees in Maine. I likely picked them up on my shirt while rubbing and rolling my back on those two trees. They recognized the buffet had opened in the porta-potty, via shifting my shirt, and they proceeded to feast.

The bites finally cleared up weeks later, but it was a miserable two weeks of trying every concoction under the sun to bring some relief—calamine lotion, After Bite, Cortizone-10, and clear fingernail polish. Yep, you read that correctly! Nail polish. A trusted coworker googled remedies for chigger bites, so I gave it a try. In my defense, I was desperate.

There is always something to take away from the many experiences in life. The Maine lesson I learned from this adventure was do not rub your back on the sacred East Coast trees, or bad luck can literally rub off on you.

A Fairy Tale Creature

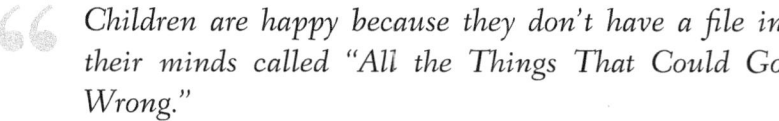 *Children are happy because they don't have a file in their minds called "All the Things That Could Go Wrong."*

— *Marianne Williamson*

A CHILD'S LIFE IS FULL OF IMAGINATION AND WONDERMENT. They look through the lens of innocent curiosity, living carefree in every moment. Our children certainly lived their youth that way; our daughter Jackie extended her fascination with animals.

Jackie was a keen participant if an animal was involved in any activity. We visited countless zoos, and many of her toys were animals, from plush toys to plastic figurines. She had a sense of adventure and imagination when she played. By the age of five, she believed she was the zoologist for her zoo of stuffed animals. She was undoubtedly an expert in her field and would even teach Paul and me a thing or two.

One evening, as night had fallen, she threw something in the garbage outside. Our trash cans were near our back deck, so she didn't have to go far.

A few seconds later, she bolted back into the house, jumping up and down excitedly, and yelled, "Mom and Dad, there is a giant hamster outside in our garbage can!"

I remember looking at her like she had lost her mind. Again, she was an expert and certainly was familiar with what a hamster was. We didn't live anywhere near a nuclear power plant, so a giant hamster would not be possible.

"You have to come see it! You have to see the giant hamster! It's huge!" Her voice squeaked with delight.

"Okay, okay, we're coming," I said as she continued to bounce up and down.

We were curious and intrigued about what she saw, certainly there was no such thing as a "giant hamster." We dragged ourselves off the couch and shuffled to the back door. Jackie radiated in anticipation of showing us the creature she had found. Her excitement was contagious. We were eager to see the giant hamster.

We stepped out the back door and onto our deck. We had a mix of skepticism and perhaps a little bit of fear, given the fact that she indicated that it was a GIANT HAMSTER. *How big could this creature be? Should we be armed to protect our lives and the lives of those around us?*

It felt as if we were walking into a classic horror movie scene. The creature lurked, waiting to devour everyone and everything in its path. We crept to the edge of our deck and cautiously looked over the railing.

Down below, our two black garbage cans stood side by side. A lid had fallen off one of the cans. Deep inside the container was the magical gigantic gray furry creature that Jackie had seen. He was running in circles and then stopping to look up at all of us gazing down upon him.

This mammal could have easily been mistaken for a giant hamster had it not been for its long, scaly tail, pointy pink-tipped nose, and rather large grin. Apparently, the one animal that Jackie was not familiar with was the opossum, but this was her opportunity to learn.

This poor marsupial must have climbed up on the deck and attempted to climb down onto the garbage can, flipped the lid off the can, causing him to drop into the depths of the dark bin. We carefully pushed the can over. He gained his footing, and his little legs carried his round body into the woods, creepy tail following behind.

We still look back on that day and smile. Though there is always a chance one would see an opossum on their property, we had an amazing moment to stop what we were doing in our mundane adult lives and enjoy the world through our daughter's eyes.

A world where larger-than-life animals unexpectedly visits your kingdom: One of these mystical animals falls upon a terrible misfortune and suddenly gets trapped. You are his only saving grace. You manage to release him from this entrapment successfully. He quickly scurries across the grassy meadow into the magical forest, safely to his family, who anxiously awaits his safe return.

Taking a magical journey into her world that day put a spin on what would otherwise have been an ordinary story. Better yet, finding a beast with a hairless tail hanging out in my trash can would have been a situation that would have otherwise creeped me out. Instead, to this day, we still remember the "Tale of the Giant Hamster" and continue to view it through a child's lens, and we still believe.

Catching the Big One

 "Carpe Diem" does not mean "Fish of the Day."

— *Unknown*

ONE BEAUTIFUL, WARM SUMMER EVENING, THE DIM streetlights were glowing down Cedar Street against the backdrop of the dark evening sky. The fragrance of burgers and bratwurst sizzling on the grill had since lifted far into the atmosphere. The sounds of loud laughter and chatter with our neighbors were increasingly silenced by sleepiness.

We headed into our home and off to bed. Before falling asleep, Paul and I spent a few moments of small talk about the fun we had that evening.

Right before dozing off, I slowly rolled out of bed, deciding it might be a good idea to use the bathroom one last time to prevent having a middle-of-the-night jolt to awakening from the cold seat of the porcelain throne connecting with my skin.

As I turned the antique door handle and opened the bedroom

door, I saw a black creature flying erratically from our dining room into our living room.

I screamed and slammed the door. "Oh my gosh! Oh my gosh! Nope! Nope! Nope!"

In that split second, adrenaline flooded my nervous system. My heart pounded with anxiety as I stood frozen, leaning against the door, tightly shut. Hearing my panic, Paul had jumped out of bed and into action, thinking a human prowler entered our home.

"What's out there?" he asked in a panicked voice.

Trying to catch my breath, I finally gathered myself enough to say, "There's a bat in our house!"

His concern quickly shifted to irritation. "Seriously? I thought there was an intruder in the house! Really?"

He couldn't believe I would overreact over a little "innocent" bat. However, I did not budge since my track record with wild animals, and even our pets, was not all that impressive. The animals took the win each time.

Paul left the room and saw the bat fly straight into our son Mike's room. An eerie silence fell, just as if the bat scene from the movie *The Great Outdoors* was playing itself out in our home. Kelvin, our cat, followed what he thought was his new play toy into Mike's room. He leaped up onto Mike's chest of drawers, looking expectantly at the overfilled stuffed toy net hanging in the corner of the room. Kelvin's hind end plopped down on the top of the dresser, tail hanging over the edge, flick-flicking as he waited for an opportunity to pounce.

Paul debated how best to catch the bat and knew grabbing this creature with his hands might result in a bite and rabies treatments. He retrieved a fishing net from the garage. Paul valued this trusty net, a gift from my father, as he and my dad enjoyed many fishing excursions together. It served them well when needing to pull something out of the water, and Paul hoped it would also effectively catch a rodent with wings.

Tip-toeing into Mike's room, Paul maneuvered around his "hunting ground" as if he were Elmer Fudd "hunting the wabbit."

Breathing shallowly, he quietly climbed onto a folding chair I'd brought into the room. Slowly, he pulled the plush animals one by one from Mike's toy net. A stack of plushies mounted on the floor.

There it was! The bat had hunkered down in the bottom of the corner toy hammock. With one big swoop of the fishing net, Paul quickly positioned it over the bat, just as if he had "caught the big one."

The creature panicked, screeching and thrashing, which caused its wings to intertwine with the fishing net. He was a fighter! Paul dashed out of Mike's room and out the front door with the netted furball. In its panic, the bat had trapped itself, and Paul could not release it safely from the entanglement.

Leaving the netted bat on the front lawn, Paul scurried to our bedroom and snatched his trusty pocketknife off the chest of drawers. He returned to the trapped bat and cut one by one the knotted threads of his treasured gift from my dad. This took time and precision to avoid injuring the flailing bat with the knife and becoming its personal chew toy. The bat was finally freed and flew off into the warm, dark night.

Paul stood staring at the shredded remnants of netting hanging from the frame. He probably considered flipping this unusual event into a tall tale, "It was a big one that got away." However, the angler's creed will fail when there is a witness to the incident, so the truth must be told. Besides, the story of hooking, battling, and watching the lunker as it flops into the lake is old and overrated. In comparison, a unique catch-and-release story of rescuing a tiny creature from a net, with a net, and setting it free into the night sky is much more heartwarming.

The Gift That Kept on Giving

> *That exciting moment when someone gives you an unexpected gift.*
>
> — *Anonymous*

My friend Michelle posted a notification on social media about her large rummage sale. On that warm and sunny mid-summer morning, I popped into my car to pick up a couple of items I had asked her to hold for me.

As I drove up, I was shocked to see her personal belongings neatly labeled with bright-pink and yellow round price stickers on her lawn—numerous eager bargain shoppers perusing for a deal.

Walking up to her, I giggled, stating, "What the crap. It looks like you are getting rid of everything."

"I am." She said. "Life is too short. I love it in the Florida Keys and am heading out next week."

Michelle has always been a risk-taker. She had the gumption and courage to up anchor, change tack, and sail to her next adventure.

This move was no different. While many, including myself, only contemplate leaving everything behind, moving to a tropical paradise, and starting over, Michelle jumped and did it successfully.

After she moved, she continued to tell us that we needed to come down for a visit. Our son Mike and daughter Katie decided to accept Michelle's offer. They flew to Marathon, Florida, to spend a week with her. They had so much fun, hitting all the local restaurants, beaches, and gift shops. They spent hours telling us about their travel adventures when they returned home.

When Katie travels, she always finds souvenirs for the family, and this time was no different. She took out her goodies, including cooking spices, magnets, postcards, and a little bag of seashells she collected while at the beach. She told each person in our family to pick a shell to keep.

A beautiful black Turbo shell with white speckles caught my eye. It was my favorite gift. I displayed it on our living room windowsill while the other family members kept busy selecting their special shells.

My father-in-law and brother-in-law were visiting us. That night, my brother-in-law slept on the sectional in our living room.

My brother-in-law told me the following day, "Hey, I put your shell on the kitchen counter. Moe was batting it around on the living room floor last night, and it woke me up."

Moe is our special needs Tabby Siamese cat. He has blue eyes that are often crossed and has limited jumping agility. On a normal day, he would use up one of his nine lives attempting to jump onto a windowsill. Though my brother-in-law's theory did not make sense, I shrugged it off and thought, *Maybe Moe gave it a whirl.*

Our guests left that morning to return home. After their departure, I prepared my morning coffee. While filling the carafe at the sink, I heard a weird scratching noise from the counter to my right. Looking over, I saw two big claws extending from my beautiful shell, dragging itself across my counter.

I screamed! The claws snapped back into the shell.

It's alive! I was immediately creeped out and panicked, not knowing what to do. There was a sea creature in my house, and it was ALIVE! Moe didn't knock this thing out of the window; it probably crawled and dropped out of the windowsill, like something from a sci-fi movie! Moe must have been fascinated with his new plaything.

I immediately called Katie to let her know she brought home a stowaway.

Shocked by the chain of events, she said, "I checked to ensure that nothing was living in those shells. How did I miss this one?"

We were both floored that the creature survived the entire journey from the ocean in Marathon, Florida, to Superior, Wisconsin, making it through all that with no water or food, which made the whole ordeal even more unnerving. *Could the creepy crustacean be immortal?*

We reached out to Michelle, who was baffled by the crab's will to survive. She said her daughter Jenny would be driving down to the Keys the following week and suggested we deliver the crab to her. Though we wanted this little guy to be back in his tropical home, driving three and a half hours to transport a crab seemed ludicrous. This creature already had demonstrated its superpowers. Not knowing what else it was capable of, we could not trust being in an enclosed vehicle with it.

If crusty crab survived, it would also need to survive the many hours of driving from Central Wisconsin to Marathon, Florida. We decided this was not in the crab's best interest.

Katie called a local pet store called World of Fish to inquire about a solution to our dilemma. They suggested we purchase an enclosure for the crab and keep it as a pet. I certainly wasn't willing to fork out that type of money, especially given my lack of knowledge of caring for aquatic animals. Their second option was to take the crab off our hands, which seemed to be the best option.

The moment the crab left my home was bittersweet. Moe was

disappointed to lose his new play toy, and I was disappointed that I could not keep the beautiful shell, my keepsake from Katie's trip to the Florida Keys.

However, I was just as glad to have this creepy clawed surprise out of my home.

Stateside Adventures

If there is a wrong place and a wrong time, I'll be there.

— *Jaco Pastorius*

It's ideal to be in the right place at the right time. But this is not how I roll. Either I'm in the right place at the wrong time or the wrong place at the wrong time.

Things usually happen when I'm on the move. Cross-country conundrums will likely await my arrival if I drive around my hometown, travel to neighboring states, or visit popular American tourist destinations.

Going from Point A to Point B via a straight line might be easier and less stressful, but surprises create memorable experiences. Mishap mayhem is the common thread that weaves together the tapestry of all *Burnt Glovebox* stories.

So, buckle your seatbelt, roll down your window, and prepare for some fun stateside adventures!

Everything's Bigger in Texas

 Remember the Alamo.

— *Battle cry by Texas soldiers under the leadership of
Sam Houston during the Texas Revolution*

In August 2021, my husband and I were heading to San Antonio, Texas, for a two-day business training. Neither of us had been to Texas but hoped to one day experience the sights and sounds of the River Walk.

Our flight landed around seven in the evening. We went to the rental car agency, selected a car, and did a quick visual scan with the sales representative to assess for nicks and dings. She launched into a long-winded song and dance about the policies, extra features, and protection packages.

Once she ran out of steam, which is hard to do in a parking garage in the intense Texas heat in the middle of August, we stuck with the basic rental package. We were soon on the highways of San Antonio, heading toward our hotel.

Driving in San Antonio was no walk in the park, and it quickly made me wonder if we should have purchased ALL the protection plans offered by the rental car representative. The highway seemed three times bigger than those in Atlanta, Georgia, which is to say, "It was bad!" The number of lanes on each side, combined with traffic congestion and vehicles shifting back and forth across lanes at seventy-plus miles per hour, was a hair-raising experience, to say the least.

The exit from the main highway merged into a three-lane frontage road where our hotel was located. Vehicles continued whizzing past us, zipping from lane to lane.

Hearts pounding and palms sweating, we made our way from the left lane to the middle, then the right lane. Attempting to keep up with traffic and vehicles tailing us, our GPS showed we were approaching our hotel. Closer, closer, closer ... passed it! Completely missing the hotel parking lot entrance, we drove a couple of additional miles around the neighborhood before finally arriving safely.

The next day, at our training, we asked our instructors, "Are there any good dining options at the River Walk?"

One instructor shook his head and said, "I wouldn't recommend going to the River Walk. It's way too touristy and not the best area of town. Go to the Pearl District. There are great dining options, and a little stretch of the River Walk is nearby. It's a nice place to walk without the crowds."

That evening, we made the trek to the Pearl District. We ate and then strolled along the "non-busy" segment of the River Walk. The August Texas heat was stifling, even though it was already six in the evening. After only fifteen minutes, we returned to our air-conditioned car. I plugged the hotel's address into the GPS, and off we went.

Paul insisted on seeing the Alamo since we would pass it on our way to our accommodations. We pulled up to a stoplight, and there it was to the left, shining in all its tiny glory. When I looked up the hours of operation, I disheartened Paul by informing him it was closed for the day. I secretly felt overjoyed to miss digging into Texas history, especially since returning to the sweltering Texas heat would be required.

We continued following the instructions being barked out by the GPS.

We drove down one block, made a right, and then drove down another block, where we encountered another stoplight. As we sat patiently in the left turn lane awaiting the green light, I looked to my right and saw a Greyhound motorcoach parked at the bus stop kitty-corner, about twenty-five yards away from us. On the loading side were a dozen police officers in bulletproof vests lined up on the grass, helmets on their heads. Each held a protective shield.

Six officers knelt on their right knees, and six stood behind them, looking like a high school football team having their team photo taken.

"Hey Paul, look over there." I pointed. "It looks like the police are getting their picture taken."

"Umm, they are not having their picture taken. Something's going on. We need to get out of here." Paul responded. How he puts up with me, I'll never know.

We soon turned left and drove toward the San Antonio expressway. Law enforcement and SWAT vehicles zipped past us in droves, lights blazing and sirens blaring, heading toward the unfolding scene.

Paul and I couldn't wait to get to our hotel room and watch the evening news. Something that big had to be the headline story.

We turned on the television and tried tuning into the local news stations. The only thing showing was a snowy white screen, like that scene in the movie *Poltergeist* before little Carol Anne was sucked into the haunted abyss.

Paul kept clicking with the remote through hundreds of channels.

Seriously?! We can access every cable network in the history of television. But no local channel signal was available?

Exasperated, we turned to our phones to search the internet for information, and there it was: a crazy passenger on the Greyhound decided it was a grand idea to stab another passenger that day and then proceeded to hold the driver and other passengers hostage.

Law enforcement had arrived on the scene and convinced the stabber to release the driver, passengers, and the victim of this horrendous crime.

Armed and dangerous, the suspect remained hunkered down in his bus stop bunker. Police eventually coaxed him off but pummeled him with bean bag rounds, which sent him in an about-face back onto his hideout on wheels. Officers busted out every window on the motorcoach and launched smoke bombs in. They ambushed and eventually dragged the criminal off in handcuffs. A true Texas showdown!

Our visit to San Antonio was indeed an unforgettable experience. Though we cannot say we will "remember the Alamo," we will certainly always remember what happened down the street from that iconic historical site.

The Catch of the Day

 Trust me—it's much more than casting a hook into the water.

— *Denise J. Hughes*

AHH, THE FLORIDA KEYS! SUNSHINE, WARMTH, AND TROPICAL beauty—and the key lime pie isn't bad either. Paul and I had that trip on our bucket list for some time, and in November 2021, we finally landed in Key West and drove to Marathon Key for a week-long vacation.

Our group of eight rented an upscale mint-colored stilt home with a white wraparound porch and a stunning waterfront view. Towering palms swept the sky with their swaying fronds. Brightly colored blooms of bougainvillea, hibiscus, and birds of paradise dotted the dense foliage.

This vacationer's nirvana was on a corner lot, edging the Atlantic Ocean and a canal. One false step would result in a therapeutic salt-water bath before being eaten by an enormous sea creature.

A déjà vu moment occurred the moment I laid eyes on the canal.

For many years, I had reoccurring dreams of catching colossal deep-sea fish from waterways like it. *Of course, those dreams were a premonition!*

One day, convinced I'd catch the big one, I grabbed a pole, baited the hook, and cast where the canal fed into the Atlantic Ocean. *Look at me. I'm an angler!*

The tip of my pole bounced a bit. I reeled in my hook, only to find whatever was below the surface had eaten my bait. *There is something down there!*

Filled with excitement and determination, I rebaited the hook and recast. Nibble, nibble—reel in. No fish. No bait. The pattern continued until *WHAM!* I pulled up on my pole to hook the fish. *I did it!*

Heart-thumping, I reeled quickly, feeling the drag on the line, the pull, the fight. *Maybe it's a tuna, a grouper, or perhaps a snapper!*

I yelled to my best friend, "Julie, grab the net; I've got one!"

Julie wasn't interested in fishing. Instead, she was relaxing on a lounger by the pool, soaking in the warm tropical rays while admiring the beauty of the glistening blue ocean, the brown pelicans and gulls soaring above. However, if I was in, she was too, however reluctantly.

She grabbed the net, ready to scoop up my prize catch. I fought with the monster fish, reeling and reeling. Julie stood by my side, net ready. As the fish approached the surface, we saw a flash of white. The odd body shape—bulbous, with five extensions protruding from the back—amazed both of us. The unique diversity of sea life has always fascinated me. This was deep-sea fishing at its finest!

As I pulled my big catch out of the water, we immediately saw it had a hollow body that scooped up the last bit of water from the surface as I lifted it. This added to the overall weight of probably three pounds, a keeper. There was my fish: an extra-large rare Atlantic Glove that I was lucky enough to hook. We burst into laughter. Julie photographed my catch, and I put the pole down and joined her at the pool.

The next day, I again felt lucky, much luckier than the previous day. I knew my premonitions of catching a sizable deep-sea fish would come true. I picked up the pole and fished in the same cycle—baiting, casting, feeling nibbles, reeling in a bare hook.

Suddenly, the end of my pole arced toward the water. Quickly, I yanked the pole upward to set the hook. I reeled. I felt the creature fighting against me as if we were playing a game of tug-of-war.

I yelled, "Julie, get the net! I've got a big one!"

She jumped up from her lounge chair at the pool, grabbed the net, and, as always, stayed right by my side, waiting. It turned out we didn't need the net. I lifted the medium-sized catch out of the water; it was dead. The pale-colored blob was a piece of deceased sea coral. Again laughing, Julie got her camera ready to capture a photo of my prize catch.

Our final full day in the Keys arrived, and I felt pressure to fulfill my destiny. Our group hoped to enjoy fresh fish for lunch the entire week. Considering the deep-sea fishing excursion the men went on flopped worse than a marlin on the deck of a charter, I knew it was all up to me. Plus, I had to redeem myself after going on a weeklong broken record of, "Well, if you're hungry, you know there's still left-over spaghetti in the fridge." Inhaling the fresh salt air seriously brought the crazy out in me.

Third time's a charm, right? I baited and cast over and over.

"I got one!" I screamed. "Julie, grab the net!"

A practiced hand by this point, she grabbed the net and scuttled to my side. As I reeled my fish to the surface, I saw it was slender and small, unlikely to feed our entire crew. However, it would—finally—put me on the catch-of-the-day leaderboard.

With Julie by my side, I raised my pole, and a stick emerged from the water. Again, laughter broke out, and I posed for the third and final photo.

After catching a glove, a rock, and a stick, I figured I might as well hang up my fishing gear. My valiant efforts resulted in catching a lot of crap from the ocean and even more crap from the people in our group.

However, some good things came from my fishing escapades. I am proud to say that my loyal friend and I helped our earth by cleaning junk out of the ocean, and she was there by my side despite how ridiculous my ideas might have seemed. Finally, whether by fishing net or her camera, she was ready to capture whatever I had on that hook.

Changing the Morning Routine

 The best thing to do first thing in the morning is go right back to sleep.

— *Unknown*

IT WAS A MONDAY MORNING, AND WE RESUMED OUR MUNDANE weekday routine. Paul was up and out the door by 5 a.m. My shift began at eight each morning, so my routine included watching *Good Morning, America*, getting ready for work, and guzzling down a few cups of coffee.

While walking toward my car, my cell phone rang at seven thirty. It was Paul.

"Hey, what's up?" I asked.

"What medications are on top of the microwave?" His voice sounded shaky.

"Only a bottle of Tylenol. What's going on?"

"What type of Tylenol?" he asked. "I took three tablets this morning and haven't felt right ever since."

A heaviness settled in my gut as I returned to the apartment, snatched the bottle off the microwave, and read the label.

"You took Tylenol PM. You need to inform your boss and come home immediately."

He agreed.

"Do you want me to come pick you up? I'm not sure you should drive right now."

"No, I will be fine. I'm leaving now."

I reluctantly agreed but told him I'd keep my phone handy should he become too tired to drive. With our plan in place, I phoned my boss to let her know I would be late.

While waiting for him, I googled the ingredients in Tylenol PM, curious if I would need to rush him to the nearest emergency room. I found the ingredient that causes one to become drowsy was simply an antihistamine. *He will sleep well, and I won't have to listen to him complain about his allergies today!*

Paul arrived home safely. Hopped up on over-the-counter intoxicant and eyes half shut, he staggered his way to the bedroom, flopped on the bed, and zonked out as soon as his head hit the pillow. He slept for twelve hours straight before getting up briefly to use the bathroom. He returned to bed and slept through the entire night.

The next day, he told me the thirty-minute drive home from the job site had been grueling. "I almost pulled over to the side of the road several times. I couldn't focus."

Though I had instructed him to call me, he likely forgot that part of our conversation, given his early morning strung-out state.

To this day, we still laugh about his near overdose on Tylenol PM. For those who wonder if this medication works well, we can confirm it does (well, not for our daughter Katie; she is an exception, which you can read about in the first installment of *Burnt Gloveboxes*).

Though Paul felt well rested after his slumber, we highly recommend following the directions on the label, which includes taking the medication at night and not as part of the morning routine!

Driving in the Drink

 When you go through deep waters, I will be with you.

— Isaiah 43:2

SPRINGTIME IN WISCONSIN CAN BE JUST AS BRUTAL AS THE harsh winters. There are days when every kind of precipitation falls: rain, snow, and sleet. Cold air and added blustery gusts of wind can cause tolerable temperatures to drop well below the subzero mark.

Wisconsinites don't fear the wrath of nature. Instead, we see it as an extreme sport. We brave all erratic weather systems by "going for a drive."

One evening, I enjoyed dinner at my friend Michelle's house and headed home around eight o'clock. The pelting sleet and rain made my wipers work hard, swishing back and forth on the high setting to keep up.

I turned left onto Patch Street and approached a section of the road where water always seemed to pool when it rained, causing vigilant drivers to slow down while impulsive drivers whizzed through for the ultimate hydroplane effect. I figured this time would be no different.

A pickup truck was at a standstill on the opposite side of the pond. *Is the driver waving at me?* Assuming he was waiting for me to pass first before he rolled through the drink, I drove forward. I sensed something was amiss. The driver began flailing his arms. Suddenly, I realized his convulsion-like movements were directed toward me.

My mind envisioned an episode of the *World News* where I was the headline story:

Rushing currents engulfed the road. Vehicles unable to with-stand nature's unstoppable force were swept away like toys by the raging water. The water continued to rise, trapping me in my vehicle. A rescue helicopter arrived. I watched as the cage dropped. The rescue crew plucked me from my car just as the raging waters washed my vehicle out of sight.

I envisioned millions of viewers sitting in the comfort of their homes, watching the horrendous scene unfold. An older couple, smart enough to stay home, began their banter.

The older gentleman says, "Now, why did that moron drive into the water?"

His spouse responds, "Wait! Isn't that Gina Ramsey? She's that author who once wrote about the glovebox of her car burning up! Definitely a moron."

I snapped out of my daydream and into a panic. I shifted my gear into reverse, and my right foot hammered on the gas pedal. My engine revved for a few quick moments, followed by silence. My car was dead and submerged in a new Wisconsin-style "spring-fed" lake. The pounding in my chest intensified. *Oh no! Oh no! Now, what do I do?*

With his headlights reflecting off the watery surface, the other driver slowly drove his pickup truck into the dangerous waters of the newly formed lake, approaching me. At the same time, his vehicle's floorboards created a small wake.

The truck pulled beside my motionless vehicle, and the window rolled down. The man shouted, "Put your shifter into neutral."

Nodding, I followed his instructions.

I watched from my side and rearview mirrors as he drove out of the pond, made a U-turn, and came back in, gently connecting the bumper of his vehicle to mine. He pushed my car out of the water and into a parking lot, stopping next to three other stranded vehicles.

I opened the car door, the whipping wind drove rain and pellets of sleet into my face—a natural yet painful exfoliant treatment, to say the least. I darted over to the truck. The driver again rolled down his window.

"Thank you so much for helping me," I said, my voice filled with gratitude.

"You're welcome. This is the worst flooding I have ever seen on this road. I'm surprised the city didn't set up barricades to prevent people from passing through." He pointed toward the vacant vehicles and said, "The same thing happened to those drivers."

After our brief chat, the mystery rescue worker returned to the lake's edge, remaining on standby for the next driver who dared to take the plunge.

Apparently, the water not only flooded the street but also flooded my engine. That's when I first learned about the term "hydro-locked." Our insurance agent notified us that our policy would cover the expensive repair. The great flood, which caused the failure of my engine, was deemed an "act of God." We felt fortunate that the "act of God coverage" even existed. After belting out a few "hallelujahs," I prayed the other drivers were privy to the same insurance coverage.

I learned that night that there were several options if there's a significant amount of water on the road: hydroplaning, hydro-locking, or taking the longer, scenic route and avoiding the dangerous depths altogether.

Following that epic submersion event, the city of Stevens Point always sets up barricades to block that area during heavy rains. However, I still don't trust that section of road. Even during light rains, I made it a point to avoid Patch Street altogether.

I considered it "the road less traveled."

Vacation
Miscommunication

I only travel so I don't run out of dinner party conversations.

— *Elizabeth Gilbert in* Eat, Pray, Love

The concept of travel fascinated me from a young age. I always looked forward to packing up in the car with my parents and niece to trek from Illinois to sunny Florida for our annual trip to Walt Disney World.

My first plane ride in 1989 opened my mind to the endless possibilities of being able to travel anywhere in a relatively short amount of time. While in college, my classes in art history added to my desire to pick up and go. With each lecture, I traveled around the world vicariously via the slide presentations and short films that my professors presented. They encouraged both domestic and global travel. I was hooked!

Any chance I had to go to a bookstore, I headed straight for the travel section, creating my lengthy bucket list of all the places I desired to visit. Wanderlust is in my heart and soul. The thought of being immersed in new places and other cultures, meeting the people, and learning the history further fanned the flames of the fire within me.

Through the years, I worked to check item after item off my bucket list. Of course, these travel experiences have not been without the occasional bump in the road, and this is where my tales of travel begin.

Not My Size

 So, wearing a corset certainly changes your state of mind.

— *Radha Mitchell*

OUR VACATION PARTY SPENT DAY THREE OF OUR CANCUN adventure on Isla Mujeres, a beautiful small island only thirty minutes from Cancun via ferry ride. We purchased a day package that offered a variety of activities, including walking through a maze of outdoor sculptures created by local artisans, snorkeling, and swimming with sharks.

Four brave souls from our group of six travelers decided to kiss the hand of death and swim with the sharks. This so-called swim involved suiting up in snorkel gear and walking down several steps that led into the warm water just below the surface of the Caribbean Sea.

Michelle and I watched our friends from the deck above. Confused, we noticed a large round object that looked like a tank submerged in the seawater, and as our friends moved down the steps into the water, we wondered what was in the tank. *Surely that couldn't be the sharks. If they are "swimming with the sharks," wouldn't the stairs go directly into the tank rather than along the outside?*

About ten minutes later, the courageous four resurfaced. They explained that this was not the death-defying adventure they had anticipated.

"We were outside the tank, and the sharks were inside," John said. "But we did see a group of barracuda watching us."

I don't know if barracuda attacks caused by wearing shiny objects are an old wives' tale, but I was glad none of our friends had worn jewelry during their diving activity.

Michelle and I opted instead for the snorkeling adventure. We figured this was far safer since all the barracuda hung out near the shark tank, targeting their victims.

The waters of the Caribbean Sea had been treacherous during our entire vacation. All the beaches were under a red flag warning. How did we know? By the red flags on the beaches, of course. Those entering the waters did so at their own risk and could be sucked out to sea. That day was no different.

Michelle and I met up with a woman who had just returned from snorkeling. After her excruciating swim back to shore, she was extremely winded and huffing and puffing. Despite the red flags and the woman gasping for air, we anxiously decided to give snorkeling a whirl anyway. We strolled up to the gear hut, where a staff member issued us brightly colored life vests, fins, goggles, and snorkels.

Another staff member explained how to wear our gear correctly. We then moved to the photographer, who photographed us in our gear. Of course, the photo was not included in the price of the snorkeling; instead, we had the opportunity to purchase it later at a price equivalent to that of a new car.

Our gear fit nicely and snugly, and we were ready to go. My vest felt like a figure-hugging corset, almost like I was instantly thrust into the sixteenth century. I reasoned that because it was so snug, no pummeling waves could strip it off. With slight claustrophobia setting in, Michelle and I waddled down the wooden pier, looking like rare Caribbean penguins, our flippers slapping the pier's surface with each awkward step.

At the end of the pier, waves crashed against the steps that would lead us to the depths. We saw a few dots bobbing in the water—snorkel tubes protruding vertically to the sky. Another staff member instructed us on how to get safely into the water and out to the snorkel area and the best way to get back. However, I don't think he was confident that we would ever make it back.

I stood there, anxiety stricken and hardly able to breathe, unsure if my shallow breathing was caused by the fear of being sucked out to sea, being slowly suffocated by my life vest, or a combination of both. I felt as if a boa constrictor had wrapped itself around me and tightened down around my torso for the final kill.

Michelle had already descended the stairs and was hanging onto the railing, waiting for me. The staff member, who spoke in broken English, encouraged me to go down the stairs.

Staff person: "You go down."

Me, shaking my head in panic: "Nope!"

Staff person: "You go down."

Me shaking my head again: "Nope!"

Staff person: "You go down."

Me: "Do you know a chicken?"

Staff person: Shakes his head, not understanding me.

Me, flapping my arms, bent at the elbows, rapidly: "Chicken. *Bwak Bwak!*"

Staff person: Laughing, indicating he understood my impersonation of a chicken.

Me, pointing to myself: "Chicken is me!"

I took off my snorkel trappings, trekked back down the pier toward the gear hut to return my equipment, and then returned to watch Michelle snorkel. I also spent a moment or two praying that she would return and not be eaten by some bizarre sea creature.

I watched her struggle back to the steps of the pier, taking what seemed a lifetime. Winded from fighting the current, she made her way up the steps. I decided the company needed to offer a nebulizer treatment, a commemorative medal, and a banana at no extra charge for the tourists who had successfully returned from their strenuous snorkeling activity.

Michelle was in disbelief that I had chickened out, and I couldn't believe she didn't follow my lead. We purchased our photo and moved along, enjoying the rest of our day touring the island, ensuring our feet remained on land.

Later, we took a closer look at our photo and discovered the life vest the hut guy issued me had been meant for a child. No wonder it felt as if I was being smothered in paradise!

That was my second failed snorkeling attempt (the first failed attempt can be found in the first volume of *Burnt Gloveboxes*). I began to believe that the universe was sending me a clear message that I should not be participating in this type of recreational activity. For the rest of that vacation, the only body of water I fully submerged myself in was the resort's swimming pool—the one with the swim-up bar.

Riding the Waves

 A smooth sea never made a skilled sailor.

— *Franklin D. Roosevelt*

WE FINALLY DID IT! WE BOOKED OUR FIRST CRUISE TO celebrate my graduation from graduate school. Paul, Katie, my brother and sister-in-law, and I were setting sail on a seven-day eastern Caribbean cruise, traveling to the Bahamas, Saint Thomas, and Saint Maarten, escaping the bitter January weather in Wisconsin in exchange for sunshine and beaches.

Since none of us had taken any cruises, I asked others with extensive cruising experience, "Do I need to worry about experiencing seasickness?"

Every seasoned cruiser indicated that since we would be on such a large vessel, it was unlikely that we would feel the ship's motion. "You will hardly feel it," was the typical response.

Based on the answers, I didn't think we had much to worry about.

Our ship finally set sail from Port Canaveral, Florida. It glided ever so gently over the ocean waves, and though I could feel the movement, it was slight. However, as we made our way further into the open waters, the vessel began to rock side to side—significantly.

Looking over the edge of the railing, the ocean surface was full of whitecaps for as far as the eye could see. As we made our way into the ship's interior, we continued to feel the impact of the waves on our wobbly sea legs. The mighty ship was tossed around like a toy on the rough sea. All the passengers walked as if they had drunk three bottles of whiskey. With each shift in the ship's motion, we were tossed from wall to wall.

After multiple conversations with people who told me, "You don't feel the waves," I didn't bring motion sickness medication. Before dinner, we purchased a box of Dramamine from the gift shop. We popped the little white pills with the hope that relief would soon follow.

The captain's voice soon came over the intercom, informing guests that we would be running a bit off schedule because we had slowed the speed of the ship to keep the passengers and crew safe since the ship was battling fourteen-foot swells.

Even while we tried to sleep that evening, the ship continued to be battered by the sea. The cracking and creaking of the ship with each swell made it sound as if the vessel was going to split in half. Thank goodness I had paid close attention during the muster drill we attended after boarding.

I hope there are enough lifeboats for everyone on this ship. Who was I kidding? The rough waters would devour a lifeboat in an instant.

I barely slept that night. The repeated motion from the waves made me feel like an hourglass that someone kept flipping back and forth, head down, feet up, feet down, head up.

The following day, we made it to the buffet. A woman standing in line ahead of us said, "I have been on twelve other cruises, and these are the worst seas I've ever experienced!"

All I could think was, *Well, of course, we would experience this on our first cruise! All the episodes of* Love Boat *that I watched as a kid never prepared me for any of this!*

When we pulled into the port in Nassau, Bahamas, I was never so glad to have my feet on land. However, my relief was short-lived, as we would reboard the ship after only a few hours of respite. *I hope that Poseidon has calmed down.*

Spoiler alert: he hadn't. He was just as angry as he was the night before. We were again riding the high, choppy waves. We attended onboard luxury cruise activities, hoping they would somehow distract our minds from the rocking.

As we walked the hallways, we noticed they were lined with little silver stainless steel champagne buckets. However, there were no bottles of champagne to be found. The lovely buckets were strategically placed for weary, seasick travelers.

We attended a theatre show after our seasickness medication finally kicked in. I honestly do not know how the singers and dancers stayed upright on the stage. I've never seen talent like that—EVER!

Leaving the theatre, we noticed a young boy sitting on the steps, his head in his hands and his half-digested dinner on the floor in front of him.

Paul said in an urgent tone, "Come on, let's go."

He made a beeline to the elevators. Katie and I followed. The lines were long, filled with what seemed like an audience of fourteen hundred people. An elevator door opened with the up arrow lit.

"Let's get on now!" Paul barked.

"This is the wrong elevator, Paul. Our room is on the lower level. We need to go down," I said.

"IT WILL GO DOWN AT SOME POINT!" he yelled.

We crammed into the overcrowded, cable-operated glass box. It glided up and then down to our floor.

Paul said later, "The stench of that vomit wafting from the theatre entryway was unbearable. I didn't care what elevator we got on."

Still being tossed from wall to wall in our stateroom, I burst into tears. "They all told me that we won't feel the waves. I don't understand how they all could say that!"

I gave Paul strict instructions. "You need to go to that gift shop and buy all the boxes of motion sickness stuff left on the shelf. I don't care how much it costs. I want it all! At this point, it is each man for himself!"

He left the room and made his way to the gift shop, returning with their last box.

Within a couple of hours, the ocean suddenly calmed. From that moment, we glided smoothly on the deep blue glass sea toward the island of Saint Thomas.

A fee is usually associated with optional and special cruise activities. Oddly, the "Poseidon's Punishment" activity was not optional. All passengers were required to engage in a total emersion-real-time event that involved experiencing turbulent seas, attempting to remain upright, being tossed around like rag dolls, and battling extreme nausea. I never saw that activity offered in the cruise line brochure when we booked the trip.

In addition, there was a hidden fee associated with "Poseidon's Punishment." The random game allowed the cruise line to cash in from hundreds of boxes of motion sickness pills purchased by queasy passengers. Being trapped on a ship in the middle of the enraged ocean was a moving adventure, to say the least.

You're Out of Line!

 I don't have the time or energy to sink to your level; you have a nice day, though.

— Unknown

LITTLE DID I KNOW THAT THE CRAZINESS OF OUR FIRST CRUISE had only just begun. Poseidon's anger had nothing on what would happen on land afterward.

We went from a luxurious cruise, minus the hours of fourteen-foot waves, to disembarking into an oversized warehouse to gather our luggage before being herded like cattle through customs. Our belongings had to be checked to ensure we were not bringing illegal items back into the country—for instance, seashells with live creatures for our cat Moe to play with.

After clearing customs, personnel quickly guided us onto a long escalator, which dumped us from the comfortable, air-conditioned warehouse into the Florida heat and humidity.

The sidewalk outside the cruise terminal bustled with hundreds of people with the same goal: finding transportation out of the terminal. We hustled down the sidewalk, looking for a shuttle to whisk us away to the Port Canaveral Enterprise Rent-A-Car.

We located the sign marking the shuttle we needed and entered the lengthy line. After a long wait, we were next to board the six-passenger van. The vehicle pulled up. I opened the side door and leaned in to load my small carry-on and computer bag. Katie slid into the van, leaving a space for me, while Paul carried our larger luggage to the rear, where the driver loaded them into the back.

Just as I prepared to climb into the seat next to Katie, an older lady with bright orangish-red hair pushed her way through the line and jumped into the van into my seat.

"Excuse me, what are you doing?" I asked.

"I was here first," she declared.

"No, we were next in line, and you just took my seat."

She looked straight ahead and said, "Nope, I was here first."

Shaking with disbelief and fury, I yelled out, "Done! I'm done!"

I grabbed my bags and motioned for Katie to get out of the van. We went to the back of the van where Paul was and told him, "Get the luggage and let's go!"

He was confused but knew from my tone that I meant business. He grabbed our bags, and we went down the walkway in the opposite direction.

Infuriated, I told him what happened, stating, "I don't care what the cost is. We are taking a taxi!"

Storming down the sidewalk, Paul and Katie quickly kept pace behind me. I happened upon a taxi driver waiting to whisk us away from the insane cruise port walkway and arrived at the rental car facility a short time later.

But we were not done standing in line. Apparently, half the cruise ship passengers needed a rental car, too, and they had all decided to rent from Enterprise. As we stood impatiently waiting, I looked down at our luggage. Something was wrong. I counted our bags.

Where was my computer bag? I searched and searched, then felt the blood drain from my entire body. My final thesis for my master's degree was on that computer. That single document determined the fate of my college graduation, and it was gone.

Paul saw my panic, and I told him my computer bag was missing. He rechecked, sure that it was there, only to discover that my original count was sadly correct. After the ill-mannered woman pushed her way into my space on the shuttle, I must have missed my bag when I grabbed our other items in a rage and stormed off.

We continued to stand in line, weaving our way through the queue, while in my mind, I attempted to figure out what I would do. *My backup jump drive is in that same bag. Since my professor had been working with me on editing the document, would she perhaps have a copy? Regardless, all the edits I worked on during our cruise were lost.* I felt more nauseous than I had while aboard our ship.

Then I saw her! The orange-haired shuttle lady was at the front of the line we were standing in. I imagined myself pushing my way through the line, getting in front of her face, and screaming at her for the chaotic mess she had caused, but I was frozen in shock. I wanted to cry, but I had nothing left in me but pure weariness and exhaustion.

After approximately twenty minutes, we finally approached the Enterprise counter. Paul jumped into superhero mode, determined to save the day—or at least give it a try. He informed the agent about the turbulent event at the cruise terminal and that my computer bag had been left on the shuttle.

He asked if the shuttle driver could be contacted to inquire if he could check for the black computer bag with the strap.

The agent turned around, pointed at a counter, and asked, "Would this be your black bag, by any chance?"

Shocked and more than a little relieved, I jumped in and said, "Yes! That's it!"

The agent grabbed my bag and handed it to me. I'm not sure what it feels like to win the lottery, but I'm confident my emotions in that moment would equate. I felt like the luckiest person on the earth! And not only lucky but grateful. Apparently, the rude lady had somehow pushed the bag under the seat with her foot when she boarded the van. Upon inspection, the driver found the bag between pickups.

I look back and wonder what drove that lady to be inconsiderate of us and the others patiently waiting. Could it have been the two days of fourteen-foot waves that were all it took for her to become disoriented enough to forget societal norms of maintaining your spot in line AND maintaining personal space? Perhaps she became crabby once blasted by the Florida heat and humidity, or she overate greasy food at breakfast and attempted to rush to a restroom before a blowout occurred. Either way, given that she cut in front of me and took my seat, one might say she was certainly out of line in more ways than one.

Drifting at Sea

 Breathe in the ocean. Last time I checked that's called drowning.

— *Alastair Reynolds*

Somehow, I have always believed in the philosophy, "The third time's a charm." My idea to give snorkeling another whirl, after two failed attempts, put that theory to the test.

"Snorkeling is so much fun," said many people. Their description was reminiscent of travel photos of vacationers floating horizontally on tranquil turquoise waters, tubes up while gazing at the variety of sea life swimming beneath the surface.

During a visit to Saint Maarten, we decided to set sail on an all-inclusive catamaran trip, and I opted again for the snorkeling adventure. In our swimsuits and cover-ups, our travel party climbed aboard the sailboat and set sail into the Caribbean Sea. We went to a cove surrounded by black lava rock jetting high above the water.

The captain dropped anchor and issued snorkel equipment to everyone.

Here we go again.

Suiting up was nothing new to me. Since I had previously completed this step twice, I felt this afforded me expert status. Luckily, this time, my vest was adult-size and fit comfortably. We donned our masks and ensured they were securely suctioned around our eyes to keep saltwater out.

We were told that our masks might fog up while we were in the water. The captain confidently instructed that should this happen, we should remove the mask and wipe the inside of the lens with some seawater to resolve the issue.

He added a caution. "Do not rub on any ropes."

One by one, we descended into the water using the steps mounted to the side of the boat.

Once there, I made a valiant effort to convince myself of my success. *Look at you; you are killing it! You are snorkeling in the Caribbean Sea!* Not entirely convinced by my affirmations, my body bobbed like a buoy in the lapping waves. I remained dubious that this snorkeling experience would differ from my previous attempts.

With my mask on and snorkel mouthpiece in my mouth, I put my face in the water and tried to make my body horizontal among the rolling waves. Immediately, my mask fogged up. Following the captain's instructions, I pulled my head out of the water and removed the mouthpiece. Saltwater from my lips seeped into my mouth.

Kicking my legs and treading water, I pulled the mask away from my eyes, praying it wouldn't slip from my fingers and end up smacking me in the face. Carefully, I pulled the mask below my chin, keeping the band around my neck to prevent it from dropping into the water and being swept out to sea.

I cupped my hand and retrieved some seawater to wipe the inside of my mask while spitting out the remnants of salty seawater. However, my handy flotation device held me in an upright bobbing position, so instead of being able to lean over and spit, the combination of salt water and saliva drooled down my chin and into the mask.

Seemingly, I resolved the issue of my mask fogging and repositioned the mask on my face, placing the breathing tube into my mouth. Paddling with my fins, I re-leveled my body horizontally. As I floated, I briefly saw two sea urchins on the sandy floor, but no fish could be seen. Whoever coined the phrase, "There are plenty of fish in the sea," was way off!

Suddenly, I realized that the choppy waves had caused me to drift far from my group. Several groups were in the distance, so I wasn't sure which I belonged to. The waves pushed me closer and closer to a rocky cliff. Panic set in. Digging deep, I used my flippers to fight the current and return to the catamaran. The rest of my group was already climbing back on.

I had only been aboard briefly when Katie complained of intensive burning on her forearms. Her arms reddened, and welts appeared. The captain offered her a cold pack.

"Did you rub on the ropes while in the water?" he asked.

"Yes, but I didn't mean to. The waves pushed me, and my arms brushed against the rope." Katie said, her eyes welling with tears.

Eyebrows raised, the captain shook his head and said, "Organisms are hanging on the ropes and sting like jellyfish."

The stinging eventually subsided by the following day, but the trauma of it all will forever be with us. That was Katie's first—and likely last—snorkeling adventure.

After three epic snorkeling failures, it has become quite apparent that I am not meant to float face down while attempting to breathe out of an oversized straw. I'm certain that if I challenge fate any further, I may end up in some freak situation with a great white shark, and you and I know how that story is likely to end. I have officially turned in my rented equipment and plan to remain on dry land from now on.

My Message, Loud and Clear

 Learning a foreign language has benefits beyond just learning the language.

— *Shawn Schofield*

WHEN I LEARNED ABOUT THE ART AND ARCHITECTURE CLASS that would whisk students on a two-and-a-half-week tour through Switzerland, France, Germany, and the Czech Republic during the summer semester at the University of Wisconsin Stevens Point, I knew I had to sign up. My friend Julie was right behind me, pen in hand. We were extremely excited about this trip and even planned to stay an extra three days to tour Salzburg, Austria.

The three professors who led the tour had extensive European travel experience. Throughout the trip, they provided detailed instructions and skillfully demonstrated navigating the local transportation systems. They also shared insights into cultural etiquette and awareness. However, we didn't pay attention to the important travel tips our professors offered because we were fixated on gazing at castles, eating European delights, and drinking the local brews.

On our last evening in Munich, the entire group enjoyed dinner at the world-renowned Hofbräuhaus. The next morning, our classmates boarded the motorcoach to head home. Julie, the professors, and I met them on the sidewalk to say our goodbyes and see them off.

Back in our room, Julie and I locked eyes and simultaneously exclaimed, "What have we done?"

At that moment, we felt perhaps we had made the wrong decision to extend our European adventure. We were alone and clueless, unsure about navigating the rail system to Salzburg or speaking the language. Although many Europeans were well-versed in English, that wasn't always the case, especially in smaller towns and villages.

We were relieved that our professors had also extended their tour. Though they were not going to Salzburg, they agreed to help us purchase our rail passes at the Munich train station. With our tickets in hand, the instructors assured us that our jaunt to Austria would be successful.

We had a few hours before we needed to board the train. Our instructors provided basic instructions on navigating the U-Bahn to return to the pension and retrieve our luggage. We confidently confirmed we understood their instructions.

The moment our instructors disappeared, we felt lost and abandoned. Standing in the busy underground Munich U-Bahn, people buzzing around, rushing to their destinations, surrounded us. We tried reading the U-Bahn maps, which looked like a bunch of red, yellow, blue, and orange spaghetti thrown onto the wall. We forgot EVERYTHING our professors told us about getting back to the pension. It was as if our memory of the details they shared vanished when they disappeared into the bustling crowd of locals and travelers.

We asked a few people for directions, but no one spoke English. Julie looked panicked.

Digging deep, I said, "Follow me; we can do this."

We took the stairs, which led us to the city street above. Directly in front of us, people were loading onto a city bus. In his black-and-white suit, the bus driver stood outside the door. We zipped over to him, still winded from the combination of running up a flight of stairs and our ever-increasing anxiety.

I asked the driver, "Do you speak English?"

He shook his head, "No."

The one thing I remembered was our instructor saying all Munich transport went to the university center, which was a few blocks from the pension. I also recalled how our professors phonetically pronounced the university center in German.

With confidence, I said to the driver, "*Oon nay ver see Stat.*"

He stared at me blankly, shaking his head, not understanding my version of German.

Anxiety flared even more. I repeated myself, focusing on articulating the words just right. "*Oon nay ver see Stat.*"

The man shook his head. I repeated the phrase, this time increasing my volume because, of course, if I spoke louder, he might understand. "*OON NAY VER SEE STAT!*"

He offered nothing but a blank stare, a clear sign he did not understand German.

Julie looked at me and put her hand to her forehead; she had given up all hope. Determined to save the day, I told her, "Follow me."

We descended the steps and went back to the U-Bahn map. A gracious woman overheard Julie and me talking.

In a German accent, she asked in English, "Do you ladies need some help?"

It was a miracle! God himself sent this English-speaking German angel of the U-Bahn to help us in our time of need. She provided specific step-by-step instructions on how to get to the university center, and we followed her instructions to a T and reached our pension.

After gathering our belongings, we followed our angel's directions in reverse to return to the train station. We boarded our train and made it successfully to Salzburg.

The following semester, I began my first German class. Yeah, taking this PRIOR TO my European travels would have made more sense, but being completely unprepared is how I roll! I told my professor and class the story of the U-Bahn debacle. The professor had a knack for drawing pictures on the dry-erase board to mock what the German-speaking illiterates in the classroom were saying. Short and stout, he proudly stood in front of his canvas, marker in hand, a sarcastic smirk on his face. He delighted in creating his masterpieces, especially if what was being said was incorrect and humorous.

As I explained my attempts to communicate with the German bus driver, he stood up from the desk he was sitting on. Smirking, he strolled over to his board with a black marker in hand. Facing away from the class, he drew what looked to be the state of Texas, covering the entire dry-erase board.

Chuckling, he turned around and pointed at his newest creation, and said, "The big state. You were repeatedly telling the bus driver the big state. The correct way to say university center in German is *Universität*."

Smile on his face, he repeated slowly, *"Yoon-nuh-ver-suh-tate."*

My classmates chuckled as I turned beet red, wanting to climb under my desk. I'm certain the professor was thinking, "What an idiot!"

That experience taught me to always learn some basic phrases before traveling in a foreign country or to make sure to travel everywhere your translating instructors do. Most importantly, increasing the volume of your voice while attempting to convey your message does not make your words understandable to the person on the receiving end, especially if you are repeatedly saying an off-the-wall statement such as "the big state."

Had I continued to yell at the bus driver, I would have likely ended up in a Munich jail cell or, more likely, taken away for a lengthy visit to the psych unit at the local *Krankenhaus*.

The Shellfish Act

 Soup is just a way of screwing you out of a meal.

— *Jay Leno*

THE WRITING INSTRUCTOR GAVE OUR CLASS TWO MINUTES TO create lists with the prompt "Write your bucket list." Pen to paper, I feverishly scribbled my heart's desires, my eyes opening to everything I aspired to accomplish during my lifetime. When the timer buzzed, I found most of my list to be places I wanted to explore. Cancun, Mexico, was one of these destinations.

"We have a spot left for our ladies' trip. Do you want to go?" my friend Michelle asked. We had many deep conversations about our dreams of traveling the world. Our ladies' trip evolved into five women and one guy, aka our "Sister Inside."

On January 2, 2007, the six of us boarded a nonstop flight that whisked us from the frigid Wisconsin winter to Cancun's favorable—and warm—climate. Once deplaning, we gathered our luggage, shuffled through customs, and went to the hotel shuttle van.

Our driver kindly loaded our luggage into the van while everyone in our travel party selected their seats. Safely belted in, we were on our way to the Royal Solaris, an All-Inclusive Beachfront Resort in the central region of the Hotel Zone, a fourteen-mile island over-loaded with towering mega-resorts. These massive architectural wonders blocked any view of the Caribbean Sea as we traveled.

Finally, after much anticipation, we pulled up into the circular drop-off area in front of the seven-story white stucco structure resem-bling a modern-day Mayan pyramid. This was the real deal, a true immersion into the Mexican culture, tourist trap-style.

Before this trip, the only activities that immersed me in Mexican culture included dining at local Mexican restaurants, enjoying the music and dancing at the Stevens Point Cultural Festival, and getting my photo taken with Donald Duck dressed in a Mexican poncho and sombrero in front of a Mayan pyramid replica at Epcot's World Showcase at Walt Disney World. In my defense, it doesn't get much better than seeing a crabby duck dressed in Mexican clothing.

Warm sunshine, gentle breezes, and the briny scent of sea air immediately greeted us as we exited the shuttle. A grand staircase led us to the lobby and our weeklong escape to paradise.

After checking in, we dropped our luggage off in our rooms and quickly made our way to the beach. Sporting our swimsuits and cheap sunglasses, we found a couple of available loungers and plopped down. Relaxed, I marveled at the brilliant palate of blended shades of blue, azure, and turquoise water. As we basked in the sun, our skin was glaringly white enough to blind everyone on the beach.

Our all-inclusive stay included themed dinner nights. Italian, French, and Asian were among the popular cuisines served at various on-site resort restaurants. However, I felt slightly disappointed because Michelle and I wanted to indulge in authentic Mexican food.

An outdoor ocean-side restaurant featured "Mexican Night" on Tuesday. The host seated Michelle and me at a table with a magnifi-cent sea view. Though darkness had already fallen, we could still see the water as it glistened under the moonlight and could hear the whoosh and swish sounds of the waves as they pushed in and away from the shore.

We reviewed the menu, which highlighted a broad selection of appetizers and entrées, including the familiar tacos, burritos, and tostadas. However, we wanted to try something new and authentic.

Our server approached us and, in broken English, asked, "Ready to order?"

"Since we are in Mexico, we want authentic Mexican food. What would you recommend?" I asked.

Smiling politely, he pointed to soup and a steak. "Uh, you choose this and this."

Relying on his knowledge and expertise, I ordered both items. Michelle felt no need to eat hot soup while sitting in the tropical heat and opted for the steak only.

The server soon returned and placed the bowl of soup in front of me, steam rising, spoon submerged, ready to enjoy. As I slowly lifted the spoon, it seemed unusually weighted. Rising from the dark broth was a black clamshell, approximately three inches wide, opened up, exposing the whitish-gray contents inside. The phrase "happy as a clam" certainly did not pertain to that poor guy, especially after being scooped from his home and dropped into a boiling pot of water.

"What the ...?" were the only words I uttered. Then I sat there speechless, staring at the once-live creature. I knew from Michelle's uncontrollable laughter that my immediate gag reflex and loss for words were priceless, giving a whole new meaning to the phrase "clamming up."

While gently tucking the steamed sea creature back below the surface of the broth, I said, "Well, we will just put that back where it came from. I think I will stick with the steak."

Though I typically avoid offending the locals when traveling abroad, I returned the uneaten soup, willing to risk being coined "one of those Americans." Luckily, there were no unexpected surprises when our steaks arrived.

Toward the end of the week, we rode the bus to the Cancun

marketplace, located at the Hotel Zone's far end. We found a little street taco hut and figured it might be the authentic Mexican cuisine we had hoped for the entire time. The menu included tacos and tostadas but no clamshell consommé.

My suspicious mind questioned whether the soup served at the seaside restaurant was an authentic Mexican dish or if the server did not understand my request, given the language barrier. Learning some basic phrases before traveling to a foreign country can make a difference in communicating with the locals, a valuable lesson I SHOULD have previously learned after screaming "the big state" at the bus driver in Munich.

Maybe the server fully understood my request, and the soup was a dish the locals frequently indulged in, but my Americanized Tex-Mex lens strongly shaped how I perceived authentic Mexican food. Maybe I wasn't fully prepared to explore beyond my comfort zone of familiar tacos and tostadas. Though I will admit, sending a whole bowl of uneaten soup back was insensitive, rude, and shellfish on my part.

Being open to broadening one's horizons, exploring the unfamiliar, and learning to communicate effectively while traveling abroad is required to fully immerse oneself in authentic and unique cultural experiences. I seriously need to work on this before my next traveling adventure.

Burnt Glovebox
Community Stories

The Rat Story
Hannah E. B., Age 8

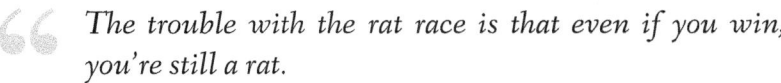
The trouble with the rat race is that even if you win, you're still a rat.

— *Lily Tomlin*

One day, my brothers, Mom, and I were driving home when my mom got a call.

It was my dad. He said, "Julie, you've got to come home and look at this."

When we got home, my sister and her boyfriend, Dakota, were already there. My dad had my sister Kayla's car hood up and was looking at something. My brothers, Mom, and I came up behind him.

All of a sudden, there was a little pitter-pat sound, and it came from the bumper. My dad opened the top of the air filter compartment, and there was a bunch of stuff that looked like turtle food. Lo and behold, it was rat poop.

Now, a few days later, it was Tuesday. I hate Tuesdays; it's trash day for me. Gloomily, I went on my way down the sidewalk to take out the trash. When I stopped at the end of the sidewalk to take a break, I saw a bunny. And I called Mom so she could see it since it was in our driveway.

Then I realized the bunny had no ears. I knew it was the rat. "MOM, THE RAT!" I must have called her at least six times. Well, my mom thought Dad was out there playing around with me, but he was inside getting dressed. When he heard me yelling, he quickly put on his clothes and ran outside.

By that time, my mom was already outside. When the rat noticed six people staring at him, he jumped on the underside of my dad's Trailblazer. Dad jumped in the truck and did donuts and all different kinds of things in the field across the street.

After a while, a policeman came and stopped him and said, "What are you doing?"

My dad said, "Can you shoot a rat for me?"

The policeman just stared at him. During this time, the rat had curled up right behind the policeman's back wheel.

My dad said, "You need to back up."

And that was the end of the rat. After a while the policeman left, and all was well.

The Dancing Delicacy
Michelle Hunter

 The fondest memories are made gathered around the table.

— *Winston Porter Griffeth*

A TRIP TO WASHINGTON, DC, FOR A MEDICAL CONFERENCE WAS just what the doctor ordered. Dr. Gayl was a busy family practice provider who was newly married and dedicated to her new extended family. She decided this trip would serve a dual purpose of obtaining continuing education and enjoying a much-needed vacation.

A group of us embarked on this journey with Dr. Gayl, including her new hubby Randy, myself, and my friend Pete, who was along for the ride so Randy would have someone to hang out with while Gayl and I attended the conference.

Gayl was such a free spirit, and her love of fresh seafood and sushi was second to none. Her hubby did all he could to keep up with her in this pricey arena. Nonetheless, he kept going along with her no matter the cost.

It was late, and we still hadn't eaten dinner. We traipsed around Washington, DC, attempting to find a fresh sushi restaurant that a colleague of ours highly recommended. Apparently, this establishment did not require reservations, which was a plus.

"It's right on the block facing the capital. "You can't miss it," our coworker said.

We searched and searched for this said restaurant, but we never found it. We questioned if it even existed. This table for the four weary travelers from the Midwest could not be found anywhere. Time was ticking; it was getting later, and we were famished.

To no avail, we found an inviting restaurant with a warm and inviting glow, which lured these four unseasoned travelers in. We figured it couldn't be that bad, as the staff said hello when we walked in! We were hungry, and the staff made us feel welcome, so we felt it was a win.

Gayl was so excited to see her favorite meal swimming right in front of her when we entered this enticing establishment.

Right out of the tank and into my tummy is what she was probably thinking!

Just like Ariel in *The Little Mermaid*, all she needed was a fork—or should we say a dinglehopper—and some soy sauce to enjoy her seafood. However, it had to be fresh; she preferred to scan the tank and select it herself. The rest of us land lovers preferred red meat, and you better make sure it says moo when it's plated with a potato as an added garnish for a finished look.

We sat at a quiet corner table in the quaint restaurant. The waiter handed us menus and told us about the special ethnic foods available. The food sounded so delicious. The waiter left us to review the many options on the menu.

Wait, what? No prices? This can't be? We were worried about what this late-night meal was going to cost.

Price was of no concern to Gayl. "Who cares? We are on the vacation of our dreams."

Randy, Pete, and I looked at each other and then back at Gayl.

Knowing how excited she was about that seafood, I said, "Okay, we are game, Gayl. Whatever you want, we will all go along with it." The others willingly agreed.

A small appetizer of oysters was served along with a freshly opened bottle of red wine that smelled like horse whiz. It was supposed to be the best bottle they had in-house. I opted for some much-needed water, while Pete and Randy opted for beer. Pete and I politely passed on the oysters. Gayl and Randy, on the other hand, literally devoured those bad boys like they were going out of style.

Growing hungrier, I was hoping they would bring the food. I had ordered a grilled chicken salad, Pete a steak, Randy a rack of lamb, and Gayl octopus. Yes, you read that right—fresh octopus that she selected from the tank we'd seen at the front of the restaurant.

The waiter walked towards our table, and we all thought our food was coming, but it was only the pre-meal breadbasket. *No way! I am starving here!*

It was almost 9:30 p.m., and we had to be up early the next day to attend day two of the conference. I would likely fall asleep during one of those breakout sessions and snore.

A pat of "What?" was served with our bread. Looking more like yellow snot than butter, I opted for a "No, thank you." To this day, I am not sure what that yellow glob was, but everyone else ate it and never once commented on the taste.

Again, I saw the waiter coming our way. *Oh boy, finally, our food!*

Pete and Randy were both served. Did they wait for the rest of the food to arrive at the table? Nope. They picked up their utensils and started eating right in front of Gayl and me.

All I thought was, *I'm starving here! What did they do? Did they look for a chicken somewhere on the street?*

The waiter returned with Gayl's fresh octopus. She decided to wait for my food to come out before she started eating.

How thoughtful of you, Gayl. You are such a sweet friend to wait for my meal to arrive while drinking your horse whiz wine."

She smiled at me, giggling. Evidently, she was looking forward to devouring the eight-legged creature plated in front of her. The excitement on her face was so awesome, and I couldn't help but laugh so hard that I almost spit my water out. However, I knew I had to keep it together. We were in a classy restaurant in Washington, DC.

I encouraged her to go ahead and start eating. Without hesitation, she grabbed her chopsticks, rubbed them together as if to sharpen them, and poked the octopus. It was purple! It had been a different color when it was in the tank.

With apparent second thoughts, Gayl said, "I'll wait for you, and we can eat together; friends do that for each other. Do you want to try some of this octopus? It really is healthy for you and it's fresh. Fresh food is the best, you know!"

Seemingly, the staff were still looking out on the streets of Washington, DC, for my chicken. Once found, they would grill it and bring it to me, plated with a side of potato and asparagus. Asparagus was a veggie Gayl and I could always agree on—we loved asparagus. Figuring out that octopus and asparagus might go well together, I considered trying a piece, but luckily, the waiter was heading towards us with my chicken, not realizing he literally saved the day.

We started to indulge in our meals. My first few bites were good. Gayl's strategy was to eat her asparagus first and then her final all-in-one bite, THE OCTOPUS! Randy and Pete had finished their meals and were drinking their "fine beers" from God only knows where, but certainly not from Wisconsin. They had tried the horse whiz wine but did not like it, so they went back to the beer.

The first few bites of my chicken were dry. I drank my huge glass of water with the biggest ice cubes on that side of the Mississippi. As I drank, Gayl grabbed her purple octopus with chopsticks, pulled it out of the dish filled with its slimy guts, and ensured it was first saturated in soy sauce. She twisted the creature around the wooden chopsticks, held that baby up proudly, and opened her mouth to take one big bite.

Intrigued, everyone was watching her, even the wait staff,

because we were the only customers left in the restaurant by then. Suddenly, that fresh creature from the black lagoon came to life. It stretched out its tentacles, wrapped them around, and clung to her face, hair, neck, and hands! It pulled itself away from the chopsticks and attached tightly to Gayl. She was face-masked with that octopus she had picked out and had waited so long to eat. The struggle was real, and it was fierce. Tentacles were going all over the place, and it wasn't about to let go. It was in the fight of its life, determined not to be eaten.

In that instant, Randy lost his entire meal on the table right next to Gayl. I spit some of my water out. Pete gagged so loud that I ended up spitting out the rest of my water all over our table. The wait staff disappeared. They either ran back to the kitchen, losing their own dinners or laughed at the scene unfolding in the dining area. Either way, they were gone.

Gayl was NOT letting that octopus win. She tried shoving it into her mouth, tentacles all over her face. The suction cups rubbed her makeup right off. Randy sat there with nothing left in his stomach, and Pete continued gagging. On the other hand, I continued to laugh while taking a nice swig of her horse whiz wine, thinking *I couldn't make a story like this up even if I tried.* Gayl was bound and determined to have fresh sushi, and she finally succeeded; not a tentacle survived—the outcome of this battle: Gayl, the winner, and octopus, the loser.

The expense of this one meal in Washington, DC, ended up at a steep $848.80, plus a tip. On a positive note, the price included the horse whiz, a warm and inviting environment, fantastic company to eat with, and a battle like no other.

Author's Note: Sadly, I lost my beautiful friend, Dr. Gayl Hamilton, on November 25, 2021, to her battle with ovarian cancer. She was so adventurous and full of life. She never missed an opportunity to live, laugh, and learn, no matter where she was. The fun she brought to so many was price-less, even at her medical practice.

Gayl, you will forever be missed. Since that day in DC, I will never eat an octopus, nor will I be able to look at another one. That dancing delicacy was for you. I love and miss you to the moon, beach, and back.

A Prehistoric Welcome Package
Michelle Hunter

 I don't sing in the shower; I perform.

— Unknown

THERE IS VAST DIVERSITY AMONG THE DIFFERENT REGIONS OF the United States. Variety is found in the things to do, social norms, landscape, cuisine, wildlife, and climate. I have traveled throughout America and experienced the unique similarities and differences the various regions offer.

Wisconsin has typical short summers and long, frigid winters. Did I mention the LONG, FRIGID WINTERS? Though I thoroughly enjoy the beautiful summer months, I dread the dark, gloomy, and frosty time of year.

I've spent much of my adult career in the medical field, primarily in clinics. I have enjoyed working alongside many fabulous doctors and support staff. However, when a fantastic opportunity presented to work as a traveling wellness nurse, I happily accepted the position. The job entailed providing onsite employee wellness screens at companies throughout the United States. Though I traveled all over, many of the accounts on my panel were based in Florida.

I stayed at the Tropical Cottages Motel during my first trip to Marathon, Florida. I ended up in Cottage #11 for two whole weeks. It had all the amenities I needed.

The cottages were colorful, each in its own tropical color: pink, yellow, or aqua. The exterior of Cottage #11 had periwinkle stucco walls, white Bermuda-style shutters, and a white front door. Coral rock stonework in a palette blend of white, gray, and tan jutted up from the foundation in an uneven pattern to adorn the structure's lower half.

The modest interior offered a king-size bed and a small kitchenette with a microwave and refrigerator. I found the beautiful outdoor tiled shower, surrounded by a six-foot white privacy fence, fascinating. Nothing could beat freshening up while surrounded by the beautiful green Florida foliage.

Overall, the Keys have a tropical climate, but a northern cold front occasionally drops into the region—oh, lucky me! It doesn't get too cold, but for the seasoned Floridians, it is more than they can handle, and a space heater is a must. Well, I had Wisconsinite resilience in me, so I could tolerate a chillier day if needed.

One February morning, the temperature was about fifty degrees. I had things to do, so I did not have time to hunker in front of a little heater to warm up. I made some coffee before heading outside to shower. Having adjusted the temperature to "scorch," it was tolerable being out there—barely—with the surrounding cooler temperature. The cold weather was too much for this little showerhead to handle, so it spit water at me. Spew, spew, spew.

After quickly cleaning my freezing body, I began to wash my hair. I reached up to grab a brand-new bottle of Herbal Essences shampoo. It was nestled nicely in the shower caddy hanging on the shower head attachment. I flipped the top open, and the fresh smell of apples infiltrated the steamy mist around me. I poured a quarter-size of product into my hand and returned the bottle to the caddy. I worked the shampoo into a lather and thought, *Oh, what a smell!*

The glorious scent momentarily took me away from the chill in the air and the spitting shower head. A stream of shampoo suds quickly moved down my forehead toward my eyes, so I closed them tightly and began rinsing my hair. Suddenly, I felt something hit my right foot with a thud. An immediate surge of intense throbbing followed.

Figuring my shampoo bottle fell from the shower caddy. *Are you kidding me? That bottle better not be cracked open. If it did, my precious liquid gold would immediately pour down the shower drain. Not good.*

I quickly rinsed enough of the suds from my hair and face so I could squint my eyes open just enough to try to find the bottle and return it to the rack.

As I reached down, I saw two big green objects. I screamed, "Holy crap!"

Convinced I was seeing double, I thoroughly rinsed my hair and face before reluctantly opening my eyes. I had, in fact, seen two green objects. An iguana had fallen into the shower stall, knocked my shampoo off the caddy, and when the reptile hit the shower basin, its tail broke off.

Those nippy Floridian temperatures cause iguanas to freeze and fall out of trees and off tall structures, a phenomenon known as "raining iguanas."

Feeling sorry for the poor creature, I couldn't help but say, "You poor baby." *Frogs defrost, so iguanas should, too.*

Using my Herbal Essences bottle, I pushed his body and the detached tail under the warm spray of the shower in an attempt to defrost him. The spluttering, lukewarm water rained on his green, scaly body and tail lying on the tiles. I hoped it would be enough to begin the thawing process.

Suddenly, I heard a knock on the door of my cottage. I toweled off, grabbed my terry cloth robe off the hook on the privacy fence, and tied the belt with a secure knot to keep it snug around me. I left the shower water running to ensure the lizard would continue to defrost. There was another knock at the door. I quickly opened it. There was Julio, the housekeeper. *Here he comes to save the day!*

In a panic, I said, "Julio! Thank goodness you're here; I need your help. A frozen iguana fell into the shower; its tail fell off!"

Julio, a Cuban-Floridian who spoke broken English, agreed to help. I led him through the cottage outside to the shower stall.

Julio broke out in Spanish, speaking rapidly. I couldn't understand him. At that moment, I wished I had paid closer attention in Spanish class in high school.

He charged into the shower stall, turned off the water, and picked up the two large pieces of defrosting prehistoric lizard. His face grimaced in disgust as he loudly and angrily uttered something in Spanish. He simultaneously launched both body and tail high into the air, over the privacy fence, and into brush on the other side.

"What the hell, Julio, why did you do that?" I asked.

In his broken English and hand gestures that included the middle finger way too much, Julio informed me that iguanas are an invasive species. While most tourists who visit the Keys think these creatures are "cute," the locals see them as a nuisance. Iguanas have a bounty on their little heads for eating the beautiful vegetation and flowers. Julio went on to say that locals hunt these critters, cook, and eat them.

After I asked other locals about the iguana issue, they confirmed Julio's story. Even so, I never expected my "Welcome to the Keys Package" to include showering outside in fifty-degree temperatures and having lizards fall from the sky, much less one dropping into my shower stall and breaking in half once it hit the shower floor.

Other than showering with the iguana, I loved spending time in Florida, specifically the Keys, kayaking with manatees, my toes in the sand, and the warm sunshine on my face. That visit to the Florida Keys sealed the deal. There was no reason to continue to subject myself to the snow, ice, and cold of Wisconsin when I could be in that beautiful place consisting of forty-three little islands and forty-two bridges, sea breezes, gorgeous sunsets, manatees, and iguanas falling from the sky! *How come I never heard of this paradise when I was in school?*

I walked away from the medical field and never looked back. Today, I manage beautiful vacation homes with my cocker spaniel Mombo, the dedicated "Dragon Slayer." He enjoys chasing iguanas all over the yards and into the saltwater canals, sometimes ending up in the canal himself since he won't let their tails go as they launch themselves into the drink. I've often had to scoop him out with a deep-sea fishing net. He is so proud of his lizard-hunting skills.

I am no longer fascinated with these prehistoric cold-blooded lizards; rather, they irritate me. Having more insight makes me reflect on the day Julio came to the rescue that chilly February morning. I still believe he could have been helpful in a different way. Instead of throwing the lizard pieces into the foliage, he should have pulled out the grill and offered to make iguana kabobs for two.

Acknowledgments

The support and encouragement from others help us to become the best version of ourselves. Through my writing and publishing process, I received the support of my family and friends. After my first book was published, the love and support continued to grow, as did my fan base. I discovered I accomplished my mission of making a difference in the world by sharing my stories. I discovered the love for writing and to believe in myself. I discovered an entire community of writers and entrepreneurs who lift each other up. What a gift!

To my husband, Paul. Once again, I cannot thank you enough for believing in me and encouraging me to pursue and accomplish my dreams. In addition, thank you for turning the volume of the TV down every time I needed to read a section of the book to you, for sitting with me for hours at book events, and for continuing to cook meals when my butt was stuck on the couch working on writing.

To my daughters, Jackie and Katie and my son, Mike. Wow, we have been through a lot. Thank you for encouraging me to share our stories and continue encouraging me to keep moving forward in my writing and entrepreneurial endeavors. I love you all so much.

To my grandson, Merakai. Thank you for nominating the first *Burnt Gloveboxes* as the number one book at your local library. I hope you follow Grandma Bean's footsteps by continuing to write and accomplish your dream of becoming a published author one day. I am so proud of you.

To my brother, John, and sister, Peggy. Thank you both for your love and support. You are my biggest role models. Thank you for setting an excellent example of what can be accomplished through hard work and dedication.

Thank you to my friends—too many to name—you know who you are —who have supported me through this entire process, including spreading the word to others, sitting with me at book events, and being so forgiving when writing duty calls and I am unable to get together.

To Julie Breshears. There are not enough words to tell you how much I appreciate your support. Thank you for allowing me to process life's mishaps with you. And yes, I'm kind of glad you experience *Burnt Gloveboxes*, too!

To Hannah E. B. Thank you for believing in me for so long and writing me that beautiful letter. I will cherish it forever.

To Michelle Hunter. I am thrilled that you have experienced some *Burnt Glovebox* episodes with me, and that you wrote a couple of your own stories for Volume II. You are amazing, and I cherish our friendship.

Thank you to my team of marketing/legal/design professionals, including Cheri Andrews, Suzanne Tregenza Moore, Pat Creedon, and Summer Nitsche, for their expertise.

To Debby Kevin at Highlander Press. I am so thankful for your wisdom and guidance. Thank you for believing in me from day one. You are amazing! Oh yeah, thank you *very* much for helping me eliminate the word "very." My craft is improving each day I practice.

Thank you to my Highlander Press cohort. Thank you for the amazing journey of learning and collaborating.

I am especially grateful to the writer's community. There are too many people to mention, but I want to give shout-outs to the Erma Bombeck Writer's Workshop for providing a special space to the humor writers of our world; the Lake Superior Writers for giving local writers a space to gather; to Women In Publishing for all of the educational offerings; to the gERMAnators for continuing to share your humor with the world; and finally to Leslie Leyland Fields for your mentorship and for encouraging others to share their stories.

A huge shoutout to Kathy Kinney for supporting my vision of bringing joy into our world. Your endorsement means so much to me. The most memorable words of wisdom I heard at the Erma Bombeck Writers Workshop were, "Get out of your own way." This phrase will forever resonate with me. Thank you for your support and inspiration.

Thank you to Virtual Networkers. It is incredible how far I've come since meeting you, my sisters. Thank you for believing in me and encouraging me to reach for the stars.

To JoAnn Jardine. Thank you so much for the great photos. You captured my personality, and for that, I am truly grateful.

Thank you to my review crew, who graciously offered to review an advanced reader excerpt and provide blurbs, and to my launch partners for taking the time to promote *Burnt Gloveboxes: Embracing Life When It Goes Up in Flames Volume II*. Your work has made the success of this book possible.

Thank you to all the small businesses, indie bookstores, and libraries for supporting this local author by inviting me and my books into your spaces. It has been a pleasure collaborating with each of you.

In addition, a massive shout out to all the podcasts that have had me on as a guest. I loved our conversations and hope we will continue to collaborate!

Lastly, to the fans and followers and you, the reader, you have a special place in my heart. Of all the books in the world, you chose to read this one. Thank you for this. It is because of you that I continue to write and continue on my mission of bringing joy to our world.

Share Your Funny

◆━━━━━◆

Want to see
your story in a
future edition
of a *Burnt
Gloveboxes*
anthology?

To see our current open
submissions, visit
ginaramseyauthor.com

About the Author

Photo credit: JoAnn Jardine

Gina Ramsey is a multifaceted individual with an affection for screaming rubber chickens and a passion for making a difference in the world through humor, inspiration, and connection. Based in the picturesque Superior, WI, she wears many hats: medical social worker, author, entrepreneur, podcast host, and family chaos coordinator.

As an author and humorist, Gina is the guru of "finding the funny" in life's crazy mishaps and blunders. Her books, *Burnt Gloveboxes: Embracing Life When It Goes Up in Flames, Volumes I and II*, humorously explore life's unexpected moments.

As a speaker, Gina champions using laughter to improve health and well-being. She cohosts the *Laugh Lines and Turbulence* podcast. She facilitates writer's groups, including Finding the Funny Ink Humor Writers Network, where she connects humor writers with writing, publishing, and marketing professionals.

Gina is a proud mother and grandmother. She and her husband, Paul, are servants to their three cats and miniature dachshund. Learn more by visiting www.ginaramseyauthor.com

About the Publisher

Founded in 2019, Highlander Press is a vibrant, mid-sized publishing house dedicated to transforming the world through the power of words. We are deeply committed to diversity and bringing big ideas to the forefront. At Highlander Press, we help authors navigate the journey from initial concept through writing, editing, and publishing, culminating in the release of a book that not only fulfills a lifelong dream but also solidifies their expertise and boosts their confidence.

Our unique approach centers on forging strong, collaborative relationships with women-owned businesses across the publishing spectrum, including graphic design, marketing, launching, copyright management, and publicity. We believe in the power of community and operate by the mantra, "a rising tide lifts all boats." This philosophy not only enhances our business model but also ensures that our authors receive unparalleled support and opportunities to succeed.

Join us in making a mark in the literary world, where your voice is heard, and your message has the power to change lives.

www.ingramcontent.com/pod-product-compliance
Lightning Source LLC
Chambersburg PA
CBHW051316120626
46547CB00015B/2261